PLANT BASED DIET MEAL PLAN

Delicious, Healthy Whole-food Recipes and Reverse Disease

(Body Healing With Healthy Delicious Recipes)

Willis Kinnear

Published by Sharon Lohan

© **Willis Kinnear**

All Rights Reserved

Plant Based Diet Meal Plan: Delicious, Healthy Whole-food Recipes and Reverse Disease (Body Healing With Healthy Delicious Recipes)

ISBN 978-1-990334-06-1

All rights reserved. No part of this guide may be reproduced in any form without permission in writing from the publisher except in the case of brief quotations embodied in critical articles or reviews.

Legal & Disclaimer

The information contained in this book is not designed to replace or take the place of any form of medicine or professional medical advice. The information in this book has been provided for educational and entertainment purposes only.

The information contained in this book has been compiled from sources deemed reliable, and it is accurate to the best of the Author's knowledge; however, the Author cannot guarantee its accuracy and validity and cannot be held liable for any errors or omissions. Changes are periodically made to this book. You must consult your doctor or get professional medical advice before using any of the suggested remedies, techniques, or information in this book.

Table of contents

Part 1 1
Introduction 2
Chapter 1: What is a Plant Based Diet? 4
The Many Plant Based Diets 6
Chapter 2: Your Why. Motivation to Change 11
Chapter 3: Benefits and Downsides 16
Chapter 4: The food 33
Chapter 5: How to Get Started 46
Chapter 6: Money Saving Tips 60
Chapter 7: The Way to Persevere 63
Chapter 8: FAQ 65
Conclusion 70
Part 2 71
Introduction 72
Chapter 1: Steps on How to Start a Plant-Based Diet 80
Step 1: Educate Yourself 81
Step 2: Crowd Out, Don't Cut Out 81
Step 3: Find Recipes for Inspiration 82
Step 4: Go Out Shopping 82
Step 5: Focus on the Basics 83
Step 6: Take One Day at a Time 84
Step 7: Eat Whole Foods as Much as You Can 84
How then can you save time and money on a plant-based diet? 85

Chapter 2: Foods Healthy Vegans Eat 88
∞∞∞ 88
Legumes 89
Nuts, seeds, and nut butter 91
Flax, hemp, and chia seeds 93
Tofu and other minimally processed meat alternatives 95
Calcium-fortified plant milk and yogurt 97
Seaweed 97
Nutritional yeast 98
Sprouted and fermented plant foods 99
Whole grains, pseudocereals, and cereals 101
Choline-rich foods 101
Vegetables and fruits 103
Chapter 3: Plant-Based Nutrition Guide 105
Protein 107
Iron and zinc 108
Vitamin A 109
Omega-3 fatty acids 110
Dha and Epa 111
Calcium 113
Vitamin B12 114
Recommendations for Vitamin B12 supplements 115
Vitamin D 116
Iodine 117
Simple guidelines for plant-based nutrition 118
Chapter 4: Preparing for Success 121

Chapter 5: Benefits of a plant-based diet 124

The benefits of regular exercise 131

Living your best plant-based life 143

Chapter 6: Essential Tips for Beginners 145

Chapter 7: Simple Vegan Recipes 156

Breakfast Recipes 156

Apple Oatmeal 157

Savory Chickpea Omelet 158

Zucchini-Potato Hash Browns 160

Main Dishes 161

Vegan Hamburger 162

Lentil Lasagna 165

Noodles with Sticky Tofu 167

Southwestern Stuffed Peppers 169

Lentil Gumbo 170

Simple Curried Vegetable Rice 171

Jen's Cannellini Meatballs with Sun-dried Tomatoes 173

Lentil Steak 174

Soups 176

Spinach and Broccoli Soup 176

Zucchini and Cauliflower Soup 176

Double-Garlic Bean and Vegetable Soup 178

Tuscan White Bean Soup 180

Desserts 182

Peach Sorbet 182

Mixed Berries and Cream 183

Lime and Watermelon Granita 184
Chocolate Pudding 184
Coconut and Almond Truffles 186
Chocolate Macaroons 186
Smoothies and Beverages .... **Error! Bookmark not defined.**
Almond Chocolate Milk .... **Error! Bookmark not defined.**
Protein Espresso .... **Error! Bookmark not defined.**
Conclusion 188

Part 1

Introduction

Let's start with a proper introduction.
Hello, my name is Jennifer Marshall. I write books about health and fitness because I believe that we can always use more reliable information on it. Having the proper diet is a hugely important aspect of our ability to thrive in our lives. I, myself, have seen a lot of people I care about suffer from poor health and lack of nutritional knowledge. I am fed up with ignorance being bliss. It is a cop-out. As a writer, I am always diving deep into the inner workings of life, and recording what I find. As a health enthusiast, I am always looking to tweak and improve my own vitality so that I can better serve our communities. If I have taught you just a little bit about living a plant based lifestyle, then I did my job.
I humbly ask you to read through this book with an open mind and heart. I have included all of the information I believe you will need to be successful at this. Use your own intelligence and judgment, and decide what you can use, and what you will just let fall away; back into the pages of this book.

Wherever you are on your path, take what I have given you and let it benefit you however you find it works. Grab a glass of water maybe a pen and paper, and get comfortable.
I made this book to be a quick read, but a book that is highly useful for anyone going toward a more plant based style of diet. I'm here for you if I can be of any benefit, and I'm honored to get to teach you some things. I will do my best not to waste your time, because I know it is not in unlimited supply.
Remember to listen to your body, and your common sense while reading this book. I will repeat that tip throughout this book, because it is very important. You know you best. Where

you are joined with plant based living is entirely up to you- I am just your guide for now. Thank you for the opportunity. Here we go...

Chapter 1: What is a Plant Based Diet?

In the most general form, a plant based diet refers to one in which a person eats only foods that are derived from whole, unrefined and unprocessed foods. This is also referred to as a whole food plant based diet. There are many different translations and variations to this diet, but for the most part, it involves avoiding most if not all foods containing animal products, and overly processed food products, a huge emphasis on eating plant based foods that are as close to their natural form as possible. Most plant based eaters stay away from eating meats, dairy, and packaged processed foods. This may be for a number of reasons, and often times the particular foods that are eaten or avoided depend greatly on the reason that person has chosen to adopt the diet.

There has often been some confusion as to whether the plant based diet is just another word for veganism, or if they are a completely different concept with different rules, so let's go into that. There are many similarities between the two, but also some distinct differences. Are veganism and a plant based diet the same thing? The short answer is no. Like I said before, the particular diet that is chosen and the label it is given depends on the individual, and the reason they have chose to live this lifestyle. Many vegans choose to be so because they disagree with the slaughter and poor treatment of farm animals, and so they so not consume these foods. They also usually choose not to use leather, or wear fur or any other animal products. Vegans do not eat any sort of meat, or product containing traces of meat. This includes any broths, or ingredients such as gelatin. Vegans also do not eat any food products that contain ANY ingredient from an animal, including milk or honey. They do not eat any cheese, or yogurt, or margarine or butter, etc. Some slightly more hidden ingredients that contain animal product are whey and casein. These are all avoided. Vegans get most of their food from plant sources, but they are not strictly whole food plant based. They may not be as health conscious, and so many may choose to eat packaged and processed foods, yet stay away from those made of animal. This technically still falls within the parameter of their diet.

Plant based folks eat a primarily plant derived diet- as close to nature as possible. But this does not mean that they are vegan, or even vegetarian. They may simply choose to eat mostly fruits, vegetables, nuts and legumes, etc,. However they may still choose to eat meat, and carefully choose meats that are antibiotics free, grass fed, and lived a free range life. Many plant based dieters believe that meat is still an integral part of a healthy diet, and so they just choose the best quality possible.

Whole food, plant based diets usually take the qualities of both diets, and even go a step further. Keeping foods whole refers to leaving them in their most natural state. So vegetables and fruit are eaten as they are-fresh, frozen or dried without preservatives or added flavor. Nuts are natural, without salt or sugar; grains are not refined or enriched or bleached. Most foods are prepared at home, or in a restaurant where they chefs share the same standards, as to not degrade any of the ingredients or take away any of their nutritional value. Many processed foods use what is known as plant fragments, rather than whole plants. They are reduced, or extracted or otherwise processed in some way.

Whatever the specifics of the diet someone chooses, if they tell you that they are vegan or plant based, you should assume that they do not consume any animal products at all, unless they mention it otherwise. This can help you to avoid accidentally serving them something that they will not be willing or able to eat. And feel free to ask someone about their diet, if you are curious. But make sure that they are willing to talk about it, and also that you listen with an open mind-not looking to judge or challenge their decision to adopt that particular diet.

Now, I would like to clarify the way in which I am using the word diet here. I know that many diets are short term, and involve cutting calories and foods in order to lose unwanted weight. This is a bit of a touchy thing, because there are many diets out there which can put extreme pressure on the body, and will cause weight loss through force or a particular calculation or schedule of eating. This is not what I am referring to in this book. What I will be proposing is that you, the reader, adopt a new addition to your lifestyle that will benefit you, and that you can stick with permanently. This may sound a bit intimidating, to adopt new eating rules for life. However, it is my hope that with my help, you will be able to do this painlessly, and really see benefits from it. You may lose weight; you may might have clearer skin and eyes, healthier hair, and even have more abundant energy. And you will help to determine just which benefits you will be rewarded with, by deciding how far you want to go.

The Many Plant Based Diets

In this amazing world of ours there are a million and one ways to get results in something. Everybody is so different, and there are so many of us it's mind-blowing! Everyone has their own opinions and ideas, and tastes. It is no different with food and nutrition. There are many ways to adjust what you eat, when you eat and how much of it you eat. There are plenty of ways to get healthier & a ton of ways to get unhealthy. The type of plant based diet that you choose will depend on your tastes, convictions and ultimate desired results. Such as leather, suede,

Here are a few questions you can ask yourself, to help you narrow down your needs.

1. Will I be eating any meat?
2. Am I eliminating some or all animal products from my diet?
3. If I am eliminating all animal products, will I also choose to eliminate the use of animal products in clothing & around the house, such as leather, suede, and other goods that are made from animal?
4. Are my reasons for switching to this diet due to health, fitness, ethics & morals, medical necessity, or some other reason?
5. What foods am I looking to keep eating?
6. What foods am I looking to add?
7. What are the overall results I am hoping to achieve from this diet?
8. Are there any specific food preferences? Likes? Dislikes?

Now you hopefully have a nice clear picture of your specific needs for this diet. Let's take a look at the most popular, or well-established plant based diets available to follow, whether closely or as a loose translation.

As you see, we already discussed the vegan diets general guidelines in the previous chapter. However, there are also more specific forms of the diet, like the whole foods plant-based diet (which we talk quite a lot about in this book), and the raw vegan diet. The raw diet is basically how it sounds- a vegan diet where none of your food is cooked. More specifically, it is common for raw vegans to eat food that has been cooked, but under a specific temperature; and for a short period of time.

The general temperature for heating food without cooking it and therefore remaining raw is 104 degrees F (40 degrees Celsius), although some argue that the temperature is more like 112F, or even 118F

Another type of vegan is the fruitarian. This variation involves eating all or mostly fruit every day. I personally do not feel that is worth it to eliminate vegetables from the diet because of their huge health benefits. But I have no problem advising you to eat a ton of fresh fruit daily, if you enjoy it! Fruit is so delicious and packed with vitamins and nutrients.

As for vegetarianism goes, there are many options for you to choose from. How far vegetarian do you want to go? If you are not really ready to cut all meat out of your diet, you have the option to go semi-vegetarian. In this case, you would eliminate <u>most</u> meat from your diet. Again, what you choose will be personal to you. I would suggest eliminating all forms of beef and pork from your food, to start. If you want to reduce or omit chicken and other poultry, then that is even better. The decision to eat fish and other seafood or to avoid it is also very important. And of course, there are other types of meat to consider. It will be helpful to think back to what you normally or occasionally eat. Are there any areas of food you are unsure of? Make sure you do your homework, if it is important to you. Including any of these foods, and eliminating certain other types of meat would be considered a semi-vegetarian, or a flexitarian.

For those who choose to exclude all meat from their diet, there are many other levels deeper into vegetarianism.

<u>Lacto-Ovo Vegetarian</u>

The guidelines in the lacto-ovo vegetarian diet state that this type of vegetarian does not eat meat, but may consume dairy products and eggs. This includes all dairy and milk derivatives. Within this diet, honey may be eaten, as well. There is also the option to go organic or free-range with these products.

Ovo-Vegetarian

Ovo-vegetarians practice a vegetarian diet, and have stopped eating or drinking all milk products. However, they still include eggs regularly or once in a while. Ovo-vegetarians may choose to use honey products, or discontinue using them.

Lacto-Vegetarian

With this diet meat and eggs are eliminated, but dairy and milk products are eaten and drank. The choice to eat honey depends on the person in this situation. The reason for including milk will vary, and it may refer to including full-on traditional dairy products, or the hidden milk derivatives that can show up so often in prepared and packaged foods.

Some other, maybe lesser known variations of plant based diets are the macrobiotic diet, and the Mediterranean diet.

The macrobiotic diet focuses a lot on whole food, organic foods, and little to no actual meat. Macrobiotics aims to restore balance by finding the correct relation of yin and yang energies. There is a huge focus on fruits and vegetables and various kinds of whole grains and beans. If you are interested in the macrobiotic diet, I recommend picking up a book from the book store, or from your local library. Of course, you can do some quick research on the internet, as well. Just be sure to check out the source where the article or blog is coming from. Make certain that you are getting your information from a legitimate source. Remember, we want to make the right health decisions because it is so incredibly important to us!

The Mediterranean diet includes light amounts of meats, if at all. It is focused on abundant fruits and vegetables. Also prominent, is the belief that healthy plant based fats are highly beneficial, and should be included often for optimal health.

Chapter 2: Your Why. Motivation to Change

Adopting a new way of life can be many things. It can be intimidating and overwhelming. It can be scary, or feel like the end of having fun eating. It can also be exciting at first, and then prove to be more difficult over time. Sometimes adversity can make you question why you decided to make such a change in the first place. This is why I have decided to create a whole chapter on the subject.

Success in any area requires a significant amount of passion and motivation. You may set up everything else in you environment, to aid in your success, but unless you have the right reasoning why you want it so badly, it will be very difficult to stick with your plan when things get tough.

It is said that 80% of success is having a strong enough WHY (and the right mindset). Only 20% is reliant on mechanics, or what you do. Having a solid motivation is going to be something that you can come back whenever you feel discouraged, or feel frustrated.

You're going to want to choose a motivation that really comes from your heart and passion. Something with a whole lot of powerful emotion behind it. For me, I am a mother, and so my daughter is a <u>huge</u> motivator for me. I want to be my most healthy, so that I can be there for her in every way. Mentally and physically I also want to be a good example, and teach her what foods are the best for our health.

Maybe you have a huge event, or life change that you are preparing for. This can be a great opportunity to get healthier, and into better shape. Some people have an ailment that has been tormenting them for some time. So their reason behind going to a plant based diet may be to experience living pain free, or without the symptoms or side effects.

Whatever your reason for why you want to do this, you should really work toward building it up in your mind. Gain massive leverage for yourself by making a list of everything you will gain by achieving your goals. Make a list of what it will cost you to <u>not</u> make the change. What have you already lost or missed out on, because you haven't changed.

You can even make a list of the possible negativities you may experience by actually changing these aspects of your life. Then you can reexamine these negatives, and see if they are worth keeping things the same over... If not, you can find a solution for them now, before they even become an actual problem.

Now that you have the proper drive (if you don't, go back and work on it until it is solid for you). We will now begin to set small, attainable goals. You will want to be able to track your progress, and know that you are moving in the right direction that you want to go. If you aren't, you want to be able to catch it right away, and correct without too much delay.

With any goal, there are a few things you will want to keep in mind, and there are also a few standard guidelines. First of all, you will want to focus on making SMART goals. This is a pretty common philosophy, and helps achievement happen much quicker. If you are not familiar with the acronym, SMART stands for 5 concepts for achieving goals successfully.

S= Specific

M= Measurable

A= Attainable

R= Relevant/ Realistic

T= Timely/ Time-bound

<u>Specific</u>

You want to paint a clear picture of what your goal is. Know <u>exactly</u> what you want. What is it? What does it look like? Invite all senses, and describe the experience. What is involved?

<u>Measurable</u>

You will have to be able to measure your progress, and keep yourself on the right track. Having a goal that you cannot measure is like going on a trip (especially one that you have never been on), and not having a map. How in the world will you know you are going in the right direction, or if you will ever make it? What is the exact goal, and how will you know when you have arrived there? Find a clear way in which you will measure you goals.

<u>Attainable</u>

In order to really achieve your goals, you must believe deep in your soul that not only are they possible, but also that you yourself can attain them. You also must truly believe that you deserve to achieve this goal. You should shoot high for your dreams, but it is equally important that you actually believe that they are within your reach.

<u>Relevant/ Realistic</u>

There are a couple variations for the 'R' in SMART. Some like to use the word relevant, others prefer to use realistic. Relevant would refer to the bigger picture. Is this goal really important to you and does it fit in with your other goals and overall vision?

Realistic can be used; however, I personally feel that it can tend to reiterate the concepts under the attainable category. Realistic would refer to assuring that your goal is realistically achievable. This seems to be redundant, so I use relevant to reflect on my goals and make sure they are something that I really want in my life. I make sure that it will benefit my life all around, as a whole.

<u>Timely/ Time-bound</u>

There needs to be a specific deadline for each goal that you make. You should know the specific day, month, year that you plan to achieve your goal by. Be sure to make this category realistic as well. Again, aim high, but be sure that it is something you truly believe you can achieve in that particular timeframe. And don't worry too much about miscalculating how much time it will take you. You may need to adjust things according to your circumstances. Sometimes when we are learning something new, we don't realize how long it will actually take, or we may be a bit slower at it, as it is not yet a strong skill of ours. Just begin as best as you can.

The goals you set for adopting the plant based lifestyle will be very personal and relative to you. Depending on your lifestyle, and what you want to achieve, there is a wide range of how you can become more plant based. Some people like to keep their current diet pretty much the same; only adopting a few foods or practices to enhance their health. Some like to change slowly and gradually, until they've completely changed nearly every aspect of their previous diet. Still others may already be well versed in plant based living, and wish to take their commitment even higher; adopting more healthy habits and dropping the disempowering ones.

Go at your own pace. In fact, err on the slower, more gradual side of the scale. Remember, slow and steady wins the race. What kind of race? The one you are running every single day of your life. This is important, and we want it to stick so you can get what you want.

If you're still unsure of what specific goals you want to make, here are some examples:

- Cut out and replace all dairy, by September 17th, this year (*Maybe you'll know you've achieved your goal if you abstained from eating any dairy products for a whole month prior to your deadline, slowly tapering off until cutting it out completely.)

- Lose X amount of excess weight or fat by May 6th, this year. (You may know you've achieved this goal mainly by sticking to a wholesome, nutritious plant based diet.)

- Find X amount of new fruits, vegetables or plant based products that you love eating, and incorporate them into a certain number of meals. (Or learn to cook or prepare it perfectly, say, for a special event).

For each goal you have, go through each category and be sure that you have a powerful reason for attaining it, and keep it somewhere you can easily refer back to during this entire process.

Chapter 3: Benefits and Downsides

Now that you have your own personal reasons for wanting to adopt a healthier diet and lifestyle, you have to power to move forward, and put action to your goals. Here are some of the other reasons that so many people have become plant based eaters. If you had difficulty in the last section, deciding why you personally want this goal, then this chapter will help you to get a better perspective. I have also included some key things to look out for with this diet, and possible downsides. There are undeniably great benefits from adopting a whole food, plant based diet. There are also downsides. As with any lifestyle transformation, there will be a period of adjustment, and also some experiences that may be uncomfortable for you. This book is meant to help make the transition as pleasurable as possible.

Before we go into the benefits, there are a few ideas that I want to make clear. First of all, as powerful as the plant based diet is, it is not the answer to all of your problems, it is not guaranteed to cure all of your ailments and prevent all disease, and I will not bash all other types of diet in favor of this one. This is ultimately about using the best quality of information to decide what is right for your body, and for what you want to achieve. I will do my best to provide enough unbiased information as possible for you, and you will be responsible for forming your own opinions and making your own choices. However, don't be discouraged. Once you figure out how you're going to implement it, this eating style can absolutely help you to make noticeable positive changes in your body, and in your quality of life.

The research results from people who have adopted the plant based lifestyle are pretty astounding. I have poured over page after page of studies and accounts where use of this diet has helped people overcome not just weight issues, but has also helped to clear and prevent numerous diseases and conditions. Most lifestyle-caused ailments can essentially be improved by plant based eating in the very least.

For the most part, a healthy diet is one of the most important things you can do for yourself. We often times forget just the impact that it can have. We are thinking from the outside, almost. We are here-our body's in there; some elusive, scientific world that we don't quite understand. This is why most people just end up going to the doctor for answers, and usually a new type of medication. Unfortunately this will not work if we are seeking true, vibrant health. Pills will only be a cure for some of the symptoms we are experiencing; not for the actual problem. I have been through this myself many times, as well as witnessed it from friends and family. I have had body pains that were only prescribed medicine... Stomach issues? Pills. High blood pressure? Pills. Depression? Pills. As much good as I believe medication is capable, they are not the answer to every single ailment we could have. And many times the side effects can be a whole other issue altogether. Sometimes, they can even be worse than the original problem, which often leads to a switch in your medication to see if results will be better. This guinea pig test can go on for quite some time! You can be left waiting for answers, collecting even more questions.

The solution I want to propose is that we take responsibility for our own bodies, and learn as much as we can about the ways in which they operate. If you are going to be a guinea pig, you may as well be the scientist as well. You will know best how changes feel within yourself. Your doctor should be able to look after areas in which you need to go to medical school to understand. There is a world of knowledge that you can acquire about yourself, that will go a long way toward transforming how you think, feel and look. So let's get discussing the benefits that are available to you, once you adopt the plant based lifestyle.

One of the most sought after benefits of a healthy diet, is of course weight loss. Most people seek a new diet for the promise of losing unwanted fat on their bodies. And although this can seem like a superficial focus, it can be a very good starting off point. It can bring a person to a healthier lifestyle, when they might otherwise never think to look for it Furthermore, losing excess weight can actually do quite a few people a lot of good in their life.

Adopting a whole foods, plant based diet, when paired with a reduction or elimination of animal products, can significantly reduce the amounts of saturated fats, and cholesterol that you consume. This has a dramatic effect on the way your body metabolizes food-especially fats. The fat already in your body gets trapped, because the food we consume usually has so much additional fat that our body must process the incoming foods before getting to our internal food storage. This turns into a cycle, because we are constantly consuming food that our body must find something to do with. The natural, short-term is to place the incoming fat into storage, in case we are ever starving in the future. Unfortunately, this is something that rarely comes in handy for those of us who never seem to be running on empty. The opportunity to use up our stored fat never arises because we just don't give it the chance.

In many cases, those who have adopted this lifestyle, and did it properly were able to lose a significant amount of weight over time. This is mostly because you are eating more vegetables and fruit (very dense in essential nutrients and low in calories), and avoiding foods that are high in calories and very low in nutrients, and disrupt the processes of digestion. Sticking to a whole food, plant based diet (when done properly) can bring about weight loss almost effortlessly. Sounds good to me!

Another one of the benefits of eating this particular diet is that you will be better able to control your insulin and glycemic levels. These two factors have an incredible impact on your health. They affect your hormones, your metabolism, and the levels of hunger that you experience.

One of the deadliest epidemics that we experience in our society is the onset of heart disease and coronary complications. For the most part, the average diet in most developed countries has been high in meats, fat, salt and sugar. These, especially meat, fat and salt, directly affect the performance of the heart and it's joining arteries. The artery walls are the pathways for our blood and oxygen, unfortunately they can be blocked up by plaque- which is caused by cholesterol from animal meat and fat. Once our arteries are blocked enough by plaque, we are in a really bad place. Your blood cannot be properly pumped through your heart, to your brain, and throughout the rest of your body. This is no way to live. The adoption of a plant based diet has been linked very closely with the clearing and strengthening of arterial walls. Real plant based foods can clear the built up plaque, and help to improve blood circulation. It is the only diet ever proven to reverse the #1 killer of men and women (heart disease) in the majority of patients.

One of the main reasons that whole plant based foods work so effectively to lessen bodily diseases and conditions is that most of these foods are highly alkalizing. The modern diet is filled with acidic foods that in turn raise the acidity of the body. This creates an environment in the body that has very little oxygen. An acidic, low oxygen environment is the opposite of what we want in our bodies. This can be a breeding ground for a myriad of harmful bacteria, and death for our healthy bacteria and cells. With this condition, there is usually quite a bit of inflammation, as well. Inflammation is now being tied to nearly every chronic disease there is, from leaky gut syndrome and arthritis, to cancer and heart disease. Anti-inflammatory foods help stop the progression of disease by supplying nutrients that fight oxidative stress (also called free radical damage) including antioxidants, phytonutrients, essential vitamins A, C and E, Trace minerals, electrolytes, and essential fatty acids. Anti-Inflammatory foods regulate the immune system, help foster better gut health, boost immune functioning and reduce autoimmune reactions that can cause a cascade of age-related diseases.

Adopting a plant based diet is essentially surrounding yourself with live, nourishing foods. These foods have the building blocks of life that we need to survive, and to grow and thrive. They can be powerful allies against invaders and destruction to your body.

There are a host of devastating diseases (and conditions). Some genetics do play a part in deciding whether a person develops one of them, but it is probably a lot less than you think. Your lifestyle choices play the largest part in your overall health, outside of your access to essential medical care or essential personal care.

The results of a debilitating disease can be such a difficult experience to go through- both for the afflicted as well as their loved ones. I'm sure that in this sort of situation, you are willing to do whatever you can to help ease the pain of those you are close to. Eating whole foods is like giving your body a rescue before it is an emergency. Or maybe it is an emergency, and you need this now more than ever. This is medicinally powerful food that can take your health to the next level. It is no wonder that a plant based diet can have such a huge impact on the state of your body.

So many different diseases can cause harm to our bodies that it can feel like there is always _something_ trying to take us down. Even with our powerful immune systems working in our corner, there are still so many colds, viruses and invaders on the body. Not to mention the chain reaction of inflammation, stress-induced health complications and slow-progressing diseases and chronic conditions we are susceptible to. And unfortunately, most people are completely unaware of how to keep their bodies strong and healthy. They inadvertently set the perfect conditions within themselves for a whole slew of sneaky little health conditions.

This is just a very basic list of some of the diseases and ailments that can be greatly improved by adopting a whole food, plant based diet.

- Alzheimer's; Parkinson's; Dementia
- Cancer; Multiple Sclerosis; Crohn's Disease
- Cataracts; Rheumatoid Arthritis; Ulcerative Colitis
- Diabetes; Gallstones; Kidney Stones
- Diverticulitis; Fibromyalgia; Auto-immune Disease
- Heart Disease; Hypertension; High Cholesterol
- Chronic Acid Reflux; Allergies; Asthma
- Eczema; Acne; Poor Mood
- Premature Aging; Excess Abdominal Fat; Cellulite
- Hormone Imbalance; Metabolic Syndrome; Hypothyroidism
- Chronic Hives; Vaginal Infections; Menstrual Breast Pain in Women
- Headache/ Migraine; Menstrual Cramps in Women; Foul Body Odor
- Oral Health; Cognitive Functions; Gut Health and Flora

Longevity

There is a lot of information and research supporting plant foods' potential to help us live longer. Obviously, if you are putting highly dense nutrients into your body, and keeping disease and illness at bay, then it makes sense that you will be able to naturally live longer (outside of any unexpected freak accidents, of course). So what are the benefits of living longer? Why do we care if we have just a little bit longer of a life? Well, there are so many reasons to strive for longevity. I think that it is a great privilege to be able to share knowledge with those around me for as long as I can. I want to see my daughter grow up to be a mother, or to become what she wants to be. I believe I have a life purpose, to make the world a little bit better because I was alive. The longer I am around, the more I can contribute to the world around me. I think this is a great reason to want to live a longer life.

Plant Based Diets are Better for the Environment

There are other, equally important benefits of having a plant based diet, outside of your health. Producing plant based foods require much less of our natural resources. When compared to factory farming, it is clear that plant farming adds significantly less pollution, CO2, and methane gases into the air. And there is noticeably less demand for precious resources, such as water, soil and fossil fuels.

Here are some fun facts about the costs of production on a typical American factory farm

- More than 9 billion animals are raised and slaughtered each year, for human consumption
- Over 1/3 of all natural materials and fossil fuels are used in animal production in the United States

- Approximately 7 football fields worth of land is leveled every single minute of the day, to create more room for livestock and the food it takes to feed them

- The methane gases emitted by farm animals as they are digesting their food is the same kind of gas that is a contributing factor of the greenhouse effect, which has a massive impact to the state of our environment and is a cause of global warming (a huge imbalance and stress to the quality of our atmosphere

- Natural stretches of land are being bought and turned into farmland all over the world. In the Amazon rainforest, an estimated 70% of land has been turned into farming and grazing land.

- Farms generate over a million tons of manure per day! This is equal to 3 times the amount of that from the entire U.S. population

- Farm animal manure is stored in huge open air lagoons. These massive sources of manure have been known to leak, and have polluted natural water sources. One such spill was recorded to have killed over 110,000 fish.

- Quite often animals are treated with antibiotics in order to protect the meat and accelerate growth or production of the livestock. Excess amounts of antibiotics end up undigested in the animals waste, and in large amounts, as in factory farms, this can contaminate water sources

- It takes approximately 1,581 gallon of water to produce about 1 pound of beef. This is equivalent to the amount for the average American to take 100 showers. It takes only 25 gallons of water to produce 1 pound of whole wheat.

The beautiful thing about our society is that we have the resources, knowledge and technology to make other choices. We have the option to go another route, other than the meat eater lifestyle, if we so choose.

Celebrity Advocates

Celebrities can be a huge influence on our society, and our culture. And we can say that this isn't realistic, of that famous people have extra resources, and it isn't an attainable goal to be able to model what they are doing and eating. You may be partially right. What you see on television and in magazines is only the partial truth of what is actually happening. And sometimes you may see a celebrity drinking a certain meal shake, or eating a certain brand of food, and deem that reason enough to try it for yourself, or try to achieve similar results. There can be a big push for your favorite celebrities to represent products that may not have your best health in mind. It is, again, really important to follow your own instincts, and decide if you are getting your information from a viable source.

However, there are a lot of celebrities out there and just like all humans; there are a lot of them who are good people, who want to do the right thing. There are also some of them that are rotten-let's be honest. But, for the most part, the majority of them are generally good people. And sometimes their influence can lead to so much good in our lives; we never would have known it was possible.

So let's take a look at the celebrities who have chosen to adopt a plant based diet. Perhaps you can relate to some of them, or their ideas behind the switch. Maybe you are already a fan, and you admire them or their work. If you like, you can pick one celebrity and write their name down, or highlight them in this book. You can keep them in mind as a sort or mascot or champion. They can be your inspiration moving forward with the plant based diet.

Alicia Silverstone, *Actress*

Alicia Silverstone has been a strong representative of the plant based lifestyle for many years now. Her life was changed dramatically by the nutritional transformation and she went on to create her own company around her concept of the Kind Diet. This is an animal friendly, vegan diet with which Alicia can share her great love of food blended with her compassion for animals. Alicia has attributed her plant based diet for clearing her acne, helping her to lose unwanted weight, and bringing her a happier existence.

Joaquin Phoenix, *Actor*

Joaquin has had a vegan diet for many years now, after going on a fishing trip, and viewing his experience as a form of inhumane treatment to animals as a boy.

Mayim Bialik, *Neuroscientist/Actress*

Mayim follows a vegan lifestyle not only for animal rights, but for diet and health benefits as well.

Peter Dinklage, *Actor*

The main reason that Peter is a vegan is his amazing compassion for the treatment of animals.

Jared Leto, *Musician/Actor*

"A vegan diet, rich in fruits and vegetables, is full of antioxidants which help protect the body from damage by free radicals."

Jared's diet has been one of the main contributing factors to his seemingly never-ending youthful appearance.

Ellen DeGeneres, *Actress/ Comedian/ TV Personality*

Ellen has chosen a plant based diet to contribute to a cause that she felt was worthy.
Emily Deschanel, *Actress*
Woody Harrelson, *Actor*
Casey Affleck, *Actor*
Natalie Portman, *Actress*
Ellen Page, *Actress*
Lea Michele, *Actress*
Liam Hemsworth, *Actor*
Jessica Chastain, *Actress*
Alec Baldwin, *Actor*
Jenny McCarthy, *Actress*
Michelle Pfeiffer, *Actress*
David Pierce, *Actor*
Tia Mowry, *Actress*
Rooney Mara, *Actress*
Kate Mara, *Actress*
Olivia Wilde, *Actress*
Russell Brand, *Comedian, Actor*
Beyonce, *Musician*

"The benefits of a plant-based diet need to be known. We should spend more time loving ourselves, which means taking better care of ourselves with good nutrition and making healthier choices." —singer Beyonce Knowles

Jason Mraz, *Musician/Activist*

Jason Mraz has made quite an impressive commitment into the plant life. He has commented that he eats mainly raw vegan foods, and that his vegan diet has been a great influence on the music and lyrics he creates. Jason even invested in Café Gratitude, a vegan restaurant in Los Angeles, California.

More Musicians

Sia
Carrie Underwood
Ozzy Osbourne
Stevie Wonder
Miley Cyrus
Bryan Adams
Ellie Goulding
Travis Barker
Ariana Grande
Fiona Apple
Matisyahu
Morrissey
Prince
Thom York

Russell Simmons, *Music Producer*

James Cameron, *Film Director*
"You can't be an environmentalist if you're not eating a plant-based diet. And you can't walk the walk in the world of the future, the world ahead of us, the world of our children, not eating a plant-based diet.
— James Cameron
James Cameron adopted the lifestyle in order to, as he puts it, "save the world". The action director believes in environmentally-conscious practices and sustainability as well.

Thich Nhat Hanh, *Buddhist Monk and Activist*
"Being vegetarian here also means that we do not consume dairy and egg products, because they are products of the

meat industry. If we stop consuming, they will stop producing.

Thich Nhat Hanh chose not to eat meat because he believed in piece between humans and all other species. He felt like eating meat was like inflicting war upon another group of beings.

Kat Von D, *TV Personality/Tattoo Artist*
Steve-O, *Stunt Performer*

Giselle Bundchen, *Model*
"We all love it. It's not only good for our health and makes us feel good, but it is good for the planet." —model Giselle Bundchen

Pamela Anderson, *Model*
Heather Mills, *Model*
Chris Hedges, *Journalist*
Jim Morris, *Baseball Player*
Pat Neshak, *Baseball Player*

Taj McWilliams-Franklin, *Basketball Player*
"I just wanted to make sure I had a healthy body because I wanted to continue playing for a longer period than most of my peers."

Bill Clinton, *Politician*
Over the years, former President Bill Clinton has gotten some mixed opinions about his decisions. In 2010, though, Mr. Clinton has chosen to make a bold move toward a more plant based lifestyle. He was inspired to do so in order to improve his own health, and well as be a positive example for change. Bill Clinton has talked about vegetarianism and veganism as a

promising solution for our nation's poor health epidemic. Bill says that the plant based diet makes him "feel good."

"It changed my whole metabolism and I lost 24 pounds and I got back to basically what I weighed in high school." — President Bill Clinton
Al Gore, *Politician*

David Carter, *Football Player*

Carl Lewis, *Olympic Athlete*

Steph Davis, *Professional Rock Climber*
"I started eating vegan because I noticed that it made me feel better and perform better. After a couple of years, I became aware of factory farming, and what exactly is being done to animals all day every day in our society in order to create cheap meat, eggs and dairy products that are not even causing Americans to be healthy or fit. Knowing what I know now, even if being vegan didn't make me healthier, energetic and stronger (which it does); I would continue to eat this way purely in order to keep my dollars out of the system that perpetuates cruelty and abuse."

Mike Tyson, *Boxer*

Nate Diaz, *MMA Fighter*

Luke Cummo, *MMA Fighter*

Many more celebrities and influential people follow a plant based diet; you would be amazed!! You might find, if you do a little research of your own, you will be able to find a plant-loving warrior who really inspires you!

Some Words of Caution

When it comes to this lifestyle, there are numerous reasons why it is beneficial and can have tremendous positive effects. But like anything, your plant based diet will not be perfect. And there will be a substantial period of adjustment. You may notice that some foods may not sit well with you. There is also the possibility that you don't presently eat quite enough fiber in your diet. Switching to a high-fiber diet can sometimes cause some stomach discomfort, or gas. This will lesson as your body has adjusts to the amount of healthy enzymes to break down your food better-even those tough bits of hearty fiber.
I wouldn't really say that this lifestyle has any actual downsides to it, but I will say that there may be some adjustments, while you are getting the hang of things. Here are the most common complaints, and tips on how to ease or eliminate them.

Deficiencies

The main deficiency you need to be aware of is a lack of Vitamin D. Our bodies do not produce Vitamin D naturally, so we must get it from either our food, or an over-the-counter vitamin. I wouldn't let this deficiency deter you from a plant based diet at all, however. Actually, most people are deficient in vitamin D. Most people are not making sure that they get enough of it. The reason why it is particularly important for vegans and vegetarians is that it is not available in plant based foods. It comes from animal meat. This is an easy fix, though, with a simple multivitamin with B12, or a B12 complex on its own. A little bit of sunshine helps a lot, too!

Discomfort

Let's face it; indigestion is not a pretty picture. But it can be a fact of life, if your body is not prepared to take on the food you are eating. If you are used to a relatively low-fiber diet, with not as many plants as the as the plants based diet has, you may not have the natural enzymes in your gut needed to process high-fiber foods. Most beans and legumes require a particular enzyme to break down and be digested. The problem is that our bodies do not make this enzyme. But don't worry! This is a temporary discomfort for the greater good. Besides, there are ways to ease this problem, and often times eliminate it.

Tips to ease to transition:
- Stay hydrated; drink as much water as possible! This will help to flush out your body, and keep everything moving along easier.

- Incorporate high fiber foods into your diet very gradually. This can especially be true with rougher fibers, like broccoli; and also with beans and legumes. With lentils, start out by eating only about 2 tablespoons per day, and gradually building up to a quarter cup, a half of a cup, and so on.

- Soak your dry beans for 1-3 days prior to cooking- the longer the better. This will break down those tricky enzymes. Soak them in very warm water, alkaline or at least filtered. Drain the water, and replace with very warm water 3 times per day, to rinse away any residuals.

- Cook beans low and slow- all day if possible.

- Some say that cooking your beans and legumes in a broth will help to reduce the discomfort they provide, but there is no known reason why this works.
- Serve your beans and lentils with fermented foods, to aid digestion
- Place a strip of kombu (sea vegetable) in the water with your beans and legumes. Kombu contains the enzyme that breaks down their rougher fibers.

Chapter 4: The food

Now let's get down to the real business at hand. What do we get to eat, and what are we eliminating? It is best to have this decided, but you can always make changes as you become more accustomed. Everybody has different tastes and dislikes, so the more thought you put into this area, the more clear your guidelines will be.

In order to get the best out of your plant based diet, you will want to set a path and boundaries for yourself. This will help to ensure your success, and help you to maximize your results. The best way to go about this is to make it as fun and enjoyable for you as possible! Make yourself templates and sample lists and menus that will inspire you, and help you decide what will work best for you. Start out with a pen or pencil, and paper. Write down what you currently eat. Try to get the clearest idea of what you eat day in and day out. You may want to keep a food journal for about a week, but for some this won't be a pleasurable experience. But what you can do is think of all of the foods that you normally eat, be entirely honest, and place them each in one of two categories: Do Eat, and Do Not Eat.

The foods you will continue to eat, you will place under Do Eat. The foods you will plan to avoid, at least temporarily, you will place under Do Not Eat. Seems simple enough, right? Now, you should do this slowly, and over time. Choose only a few foods to adopt, and to eliminate from your diet at a time. This will be a gradual transition. You may even want to make a third category marked Why? This category is a great place to note why you are choosing to add or eliminate that food, in case you need a reminder.

Here are some examples of **foods to add** (Do Eat, or whatever you decide to name it)

Vegetables

Kale

Broccoli

Cucumber

Celery

Ginger

Sweet Potato

Bell Peppers

Carrots

Corn

Cucumbers

Garlic

Ginger

Mushrooms

Onions

Potatoes

Tomatoes (technically fruit)

Avocado (also a fruit)

Zucchini

Fruit

Banana

Apple

Orange

Grapefruit

Grapes

Pineapple

Berries

Lemons and Limes

Pears

Grains

Brown Rice

Sprouted or Gluten Free Bread

Rice or gluten free Noodles

Quinoia

Steel Cut Oats

Tortillas or Taco shells

Proteins

Tofu

Tempeh

Beans

Lintels

Nuts

Nut Butters

Seeds

Chia Seeds

Chickpeas

Edamame

Flax Seed

Hummus

Quinoia

Tahini

(Dark Leafy Green Vegetables)

Frozen Foods

Dairy-free ice cream/ sorbets

Frozen Veggies

Frozen Fruit

Condiments

Hot Sauce

Ketchup

Tahini

Soy Sauce

Canned Goods

Beans

Coconut Milk

Tomatoes

Tomato Paste

Pantry Essentials

Bouillon Cubes

Dried Fruit

Nutritional Yeast

Oils

Olives

Marinara Sauce

Vinegars

Agave Syrup

Vanilla Extract

Baking Soda

Baking Powder

Chocolate, dark or dairy free

Cocoa powder, unsweetened

Sugar

Flour

Maple Syrup

<u>Spices</u>

Basil

Black Pepper

Chili Powder

Ground Cinnamon

Ground Cumin

Curry Powder

Garam Masala

Garlic Powder

Onion Powder

Oregano

Paprika

Rosemary

Salt (iodized)

Ground Turmeric

Thyme

Foods to Eliminate

Adding the right life-supporting foods to your life will go a long way toward helping you achieve the health you desire. It will give you the nutrients and enzymes to make your body work harmoniously. However adding helpful foods is only part of the food equation. Your body is constantly working to build healthy cells, and to discard of the dead unhealthy material. This process of detoxification is an essential body function. It protects us against destructive toxins and damaged cells. Left unchecked without being removed these toxins can wreak havoc on your, and has the potential to destroy perfectly healthy cells and organs. The detoxification process is just as important as eating nutrient rich foods. The absolute best way to remove unhealthy foods and harmful toxins from your body is to avoid eating them in the first place.

I have composed a basic list of foods and ingredients that should be removed from your kitchen, and your everyday diet. Eliminating these foods will help you achieve the cleanest possible dietary health.

Reduce or Eliminate:

All animal products

Honey (if going full vegan, or eliminating for any reason)

Dairy products

High fructose corn syrup (All refined sugars)

Partially hydrogenated oils

Enriched/ bleached flours

Foods with a very long list of unnatural ingredients

Monosodium glutamate

Foods enriched or fortified with unnatural vitamins

*This happens when the food has been extracted, and separated from its natural state. It is then usually added with essential trace elements and vitamins. This is not the way we want to consume our food.

Side note: Usually the fact that foods that have long scientific sounding ingredients means that they were made in a lab. This doesn't fair well once in the body.

Learning to Read Labels

Adopting a new eating style and becoming more aware of what is coming into your body can be a pretty overwhelming endeavor. But with the right knowledge and a lot of practice, you will be able to find out what is in anything you are eating, and you will be able to decide for yourself if it is something that you will choose to eat. The first step to improving something is awareness. Once you have a better idea of what goes into your food, you can move away from the unnatural foods and closer to natural, wholesome nutrition.

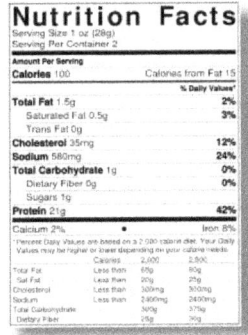

Here I have included a brief lesson on deciphering your nutritional facts.

For many people, the nutritional facts on a food means very little, when it comes to making food choices. For one, it can be a challenge to understand exactly how nutritional information correlates to what is going on in your body. I think that the number or calories is probably at the most basic level understanding how to use food labels. Basically, you need a certain amount of calories per day, to maintain your body weight and current level of nutrition. Your body uses a certain range of calories daily, just by being alive and moving around. The more physical activity you get, the more calories are burned. The more calorie-filled foods you eat, the more calories are stored in your body, usually as fat. Having more muscle on your body means that you can burn more fat.

There are, of course, many other factors that come into play when your body metabolizes food.

<u>Macros & Vitamins</u>

Another basic gauge for judging your food's nutritional value is the division or macros. What is your meal primarily composed of? This is referring to the type of food, and how it will generally be used in the body. Fat, protein and carbohydrates make up your macros. Also important are the amount of sugar and the amount of salt.

<u>Fat</u>

Fat is either used immediately in the presence of physical activity, or it will be stored as fat in the body. Fat is stored up in case we are ever faced with a food shortage and need to be protected against starvation. In most developed countries, unless you have a specific life complication where you go hungry often, we do not have a food shortage. We have a surplus of calorie-dense food that is devoid of any nutrition. This is where much of our excess fat comes from.

But all fats are not created equal. Our bodies actually really need fat to be healthy, lustrous, and to feel satisfied by our meals. You want to get plenty of good fats in your diet to keep the right balance. Healthy fats are unrefined, and come mostly from plants, nuts and seeds. Truth be told, healthy fats can also be found in certain types of fish and seafood. Things like avocados and coconut oil provide wonderful healthy fats. So do nuts and seeds like flax and chia. Snack on plenty of nuts and seeds!

<u>Protein:</u>

This nutrient is the main ingredient to building our cells and muscles. Protein is what gives us our lean, powerful muscles. Protein helps us to metabolize fat, and helps to regulate your blood sugar. It also benefits your physical performance abilities, not to mention it also really helps to fill you up without having to eat a lot of extra calories. With the right combination, you can make protein work for you to create the body and the health you strive for.

Carbohydrates

This is essentially your sugar, for your physical energy. Your carbohydrates are either filled with a good source of fiber, or turned into sugar- to be used immediately, or stored as fat.

When it comes to the ingredients list, the first 5 ingredients make up most of that food, and contain about 95% of the whole. All ingredients descend in order of concentration. Look out for chemical-laden ingredients which are hard to pronounce, and sound unfamiliar or not descriptive of what it is originally derived from. Look for whole ingredients that are un-tampered with. And if you choose to eat something you know has unhealthy ingredients, then make sure you enjoy it, count it as a treat (or cheat meal), and make up for it moving forward at the next meal.

I also want you to be aware of the order in which your food is digested. Different foods have different schedules of when they enter and exit the body. They also require different enzymes and ph balances to be properly digested. Now, if you have quite a strong gut, you may not need this step. But if you are experiencing noticeable digestive issues, then food combining may make a big difference for you.

Here is a general guideline for combining your foods effectively and each foods approximate digestion time

Eat melon alone (takes 15-30 minutes)

Eat fruits alone (1-2 hours)

Starches like grains, roots, beans, and bread items can be eaten with vegetables (3 hours)

Proteins like nuts, seeds beans and meat go great with vegetables (4 hours, but animal protein can take 8 hours or longer)

Avoid mixing protein and starched. They do not work well together.

Avoid mixing fruit and protein- or starch and fruit. This can create rotting in the gut.

Enjoy avocados with just about anything!

Veggies are compatible with anything!

Special Diets & Substitutions

If you have a specific food allergy, you know the importance scanning your food ingredients, and assuring it isn't there. One of the great things about the plant based diet is that you can adapt it, and you don't have to stick to a specific set of meals to get the positive results. You can make substitutions, or a different recipe altogether, if you can't find a way around that particular ingredient.

Common Food Allergies

Peanuts

Tree nuts

Milk

Eggs

Fish

Shellfish

Coconut Oil (some auto-immune diseases)

Gluten, Wheat or Certain Grains (Celiac Disease)

Chapter 5: How to Get Started

This chapter will teach you how to put everything into action.

In order to get started on the right foot, you'll need to get into the right headspace for the changes you are incorporating into your life. Having the right mindset for change and for your health will go a long way to help you to be effective and successful at this.

It is amazing just trying to imagine the amount of power your mental state and thoughts can have on your life, and on your decisions. How do we assure that your mind is working on your side? By guiding your opinions and perceptions. And by trying consciously to maintain a positive attitude. Just an overall willingness to do what it will take. You must find, and hold, the strength to commit to new habits; replacing old ones. You are making a commitment to tread into territory that is mysterious to you. You need to be open to fail a little, and try something new.

The plant based diet can have a lot of different connotations along with it. Sometimes having a strong misconception can be a roadblock, if you let it color your beliefs and choices. Try to keep an open mind going into this change. Many people have the perception that, for example, vegan food is tasteless. Or that this type of eating has to be difficult. You may agree, or think that it is impossible to get the proper nutrients on a plant based diet. Many people also believe that eating this way must be super expensive. You will find your own path and beliefs as you learn to experiment more. I will give you all of the tools that I can, but you have to be willing to explore and experiment to find your path.

There are many ways to go about change, and what you choose will be based on a variety of things. Some people prefer to transition very slowly in order to make the adjustment not such a shock, and also to pay more attention to the process over long term. Others like to completely change their life over the course of a month, week or even overnight. Some people have a lot of fears revolving around change, and some people may have a sense of urgency around the subject, because of a certain upcoming event with a specific date.

The method I prefer, and the one I will discuss in this book, is the steady, gradual change that has a clear direction and purpose. I find that this is the best way to build solid habits, and a stronger foundation under your new construction of healthy habits. Let's get down to it!

Stocking the Kitchen

I want you to think of your kitchen as your strongest ally on the road to greater health. Are you inspired? Feel free to switch up the décor in your kitchen to make it more meaningful, and to make it more conducive to preparing and eating healthy meals. You want to feel inspired, and in control of yourself when you walk in the kitchen to create a meal or grab a snack. If you find that you don't have everything that you need to have the experience, you can plan to slowly gather acquire these items over time; and improvise the rest. While you are making the transition to vegetable proteins, be sure to check out the many types of mock meats, or textured vegetable proteins available. Yes, some may be overly processes, but it can definitely be a great alternative to animal meats. This can be especially helpful when you are just starting to make the transition. Once you are accustomed to not eating meat, or eating very little, you can start to move away from the more processed versions and move toward more wholesome options.

I will give you a glance at what I recommend stock the house with in order to get the best results and to enjoy some pretty delicious food!

What to keep in the kitchen

It may be tempting to just go into your kitchen and toss everything out, starting from scratch. More than likely, though, you still have some foods that are worth keeping around. Take a look in there, and acknowledge the foods you have that are beneficial for you. Everything else can go. It may be more enjoyable to enlist a helper for this job, or you may want to tackle it all yourself like a nutritional warrior. Either way, we are going to separate the good from the ugly. I like to start in the pantry and cupboards, pull every single item out, put it on the table or counter and begin sorting objectively. You can separate the food you are eliminating into 3 categories- toss; pass on and donate. You can pass any items on that you thing a friend or family member will use (this can also be nice for when an item is open, but still good. Any unclaimed food that is still in good condition can be donated to a local shelter or food closet.

Kitchen appliances and tools

Blender

Good Pan

Cutting boards

Mixing bowls

Good knife

Food storage containers

Baking Sheet

Colander

Spiralizer

Vegetable peeler

Can opener

Garlic press

Mandolin slicer

Juicer

Citrus Juicer

Meal Planning

For this next step, it may be beneficial for you to first spend some time recording what you normally eat day to day. I would do this for two weeks, while tracking calories as well. This will give you a good idea of the type of foods you typically eat. You can find your average daily calories and decide what adjustments need to be made.

Leave an allowance of one page for each day, and write down everything you ate (time would be helpful here too, but don't worry if you're not quite ready for that yet). Also include what meals you ate them for and the calories (if you are tracking calories). Remember: Make sure to record EVERYTHING that you eat. This is important.

Next take that information and analyze it. What are your go-to foods? Are you eating calories way beyond your needs? Way less? Do you tend to lean toward sweets & sugary foods? Or how about spicy or salty? If you are recording times of your meals, ask yourself how often you get hungry. Note the size of your meals, how often you get hungry, when you are at your hungriest, and when you crave to snack.

Once you have recorded in your food journal for two weeks, and you have gathered the information you need, you can make the necessary adjustments. What food did you eat, that you will be eliminating from your diet. Are there any go-to foods that you need to substitute for something healthier? Are there any flavors that you love, but need a better version for? You really can collect so much information from this little bit of data collecting.

Now we will work on building menu plans for you.

If you are still wanting to track your calories, and assuming you are eating 3 meals and 2 snacks per day, you will take your target daily calories and divide it by 4. This will give you the value of each of your 3 meals. Next divide that number by 2, and you have the value for each of your snacks. Now this will be a general guideline for how many calories should be in each meal and snack.

So for example, say you are eating 1,200 calories a day (this is only an example. Keep in mind that this is the minimum amount of calories an adult should have daily, and it is recommended for those of us who are around 5', like me).

You would divide that number by 4, which is 300. So each meal would be 300 calories. Divide that number by 2, and you get 150. So each snack would be 150 calories.

Use this guideline during the meal planning process. You can decide whether you like to meal plan better on paper, or on a computer word document. I like to do a little bit of both. Also, experiment with formats to find what suits you. For each day of the week, leave a space for breakfast, lunch, and dinner with 2 snacks (also the occasional dessert!). It is also helpful to plan out your beverages, if you are looking to improve that as well. But you can allow yourself unlimited pure water and unsweetened tea. Keep in mind, black tea is much more acidic. I tend to stick with variations of green tea.

As an extra tip, I find it really helps to repeat as many of my meals day-to-day, as possible, while still enjoying those meals. It can really work to reduce the amount of time and effort planning and prepping them. Also tracking their calories will be easier.

Planning Meals & Writing the Shopping List

Create a word document or grab a pen and some paper, and make a quick shopping list of what you need. What groceries are running low? Next brainstorm meals that you want to have for the week. Take a glance through local store deals, coupons, and sales.

You may find it easier to build your menu plan starting with you dinners. This can sometimes be beneficial, especially when you tend to have dinner with family, friends, colleagues or your significant other. If this isn't your family dynamic, no worries! You can choose what meals you would like to start with, and fill in the other meals and snacks until you have a plan for all of your meals for the week. Just being this prepared can make life so much easier, and assure you will be prepared to make healthier food choices.

Find out what you need to buy for your meals and add them to your grocery list.

Here is a sample menu plan for the week, and a companion grocery list:

Monday

Breakfast: Oatmeal; Fruit

Lunch: Vegan Chili; bread

Dinner: Veggie teriyaki with rice

Snacks: Fruit; Granola; Nuts

Tuesday

Breakfast: Tofu scramble; Veggies

Lunch: Burrito Bowl

Dinner: Lentil Stew

Snacks: Fruit; Trail Mix; Veggies and Hummus

Wednesday

Breakfast: Oatmeal; Fruit

Lunch: Veggie Sushi Rolls

Dinner: Tacos; Beans and Rice

Snacks: Fruit; Dark Chocolate; Seeds

Thursday

Breakfast: Smoothie Bowl

Lunch: Veggie Wrap

Dinner: Veggie Burgers and Homemade French Fries

Snacks: Fruit; Dried Veggies; Veggie and Hummus

Friday

Breakfast: Tofu Scramble, veggies

Lunch: Sprouted Grain Veggie Sandwich

Dinner: Veggie Teriyaki with Tofu

Snacks: Fruit; Trail Mix; Granola

Saturday

Breakfast: Breakfast Wrap

Lunch: Veggie Wrap

Dinner: Lentil Stew

Snacks: Fruit; Veggies and Dip; Wine

Sunday

Breakfast: Green Smoothie

Lunch: Sprouted Grain Sandwich

Dinner: Veggie Burgers with Homemade French Fries

Snacks: Fruit; Granola; A Special Dessert Item for once a week

Making Your Grocery List

Fruit:

Apples

Bananas

Cucumber

Pineapple

Watermelon

Lemon or Lime

Vegetables

Lettuce

Tomatoes

Onions

Carrots

Celery

Cucumbers

Avocados

Broccoli

Cauliflower

Potatoes

Garlic

Spinach

Refrigerated/ Dairy or Alternatives:

Soymilk/ milk

Margarine

Hummus (or you can make your own)

Tofu

Canned Goods:

Pineapple

Refried Beans

Garbanzo Beans

Tomatoes

Tomato paste

Dry Goods:

Rice

Nori Sheets (for sushi)

Oatmeal

Sea Salt

Dark Chocolate

Spices

Granola

Nuts

Seeds

Dried Veggies

Spices

Lentils

Beans

Bread/ Cereal:

Oatmeal

Pita Bread

Wrap or tortilla

Sprouted Grain Bread

Frozen Foods:

Edamame

Spinach

Strawberries

Etc:

Vegan Mayonnaise (or use hummus)

Ketchup

Hot Sauce

Soy sauce

Hoisin Sauce

Honey

Optional:

Wine

Special Dessert

Chapter 6: Money Saving Tips

One of the reasons some people give for not eating healthy, whole ingredient foods, is that they believe it will be too expensive to maintain. And it can be true to a certain extent. It can be tricky to find good-quality organic produce for a low cost. And sometimes they less expensive stores do not have the best selection of quality fruits and vegetables. I have experienced this for myself, and have found ways to get the most for my money. First of all, I remember where I can get the best deal each item. You can make a note of this, or start a word document to help you keep track of your money saving strategies. I like to buy some of my heartier, less fussy produce at a more inexpensive store, and go to the more higher-end health food-friendly stores for my more finicky foods-like berries, and peaches. Shopping around at too many different stores can make things more complicated, but picking a few stores that tend to compete may be in your best interest.

There are many ways that you can save money while still eating wholesome foods. Some of them may work perfectly well for you, and others you can discard.

One of the best ways to avoid extra costs is to plan your meals ahead of time. This will give you a better sense of control and preparation for the week ahead, which will cut down on extra trips to the store. You can plan a certain day of the week to batch your grocery store trips.

Another highly effective way to reduce unnecessary and unhealthy purchases is to make sure that you are not hungry when you go food shopping. Actually, I don't recommend doing any kind of shopping hungry-it's just not pleasant. I know eating before grocery shopping is not a new suggestion, but it is worth repeating. It works. Every time I go to the grocery store hungry, I end up with more snacks and sweet treats in my cart, on top of the meal I plan to eat when I get home; most of the time they are foods that I wouldn't have picked up, had I eaten a proper meal beforehand. So if possible, eat at least a little something before you take on the grocery store.

It can be in your benefit to scan through the sales of your local stores, to see if there is some extra money to save on the groceries you already plan to buy. This is key- seeing items being on sale (even a really great sale) do not mean that you should buy foods that you don't need and weren't already buying. Some stores provide a club with loyalty rewards. You can take advantage of these and plan your shopping list around it. For items that aren't on sale, you can sometimes find coupons that can really help lower your overall cost. (Again, only use coupons for items you are planning to buy already. Unnecessary costs, even if at a discount, still cost you extra money.) Store apps may be worth looking into, as well. They can notify you when there is a sale, or certain foods that have been discounted.

Sometimes you can find better deals for the amount of food you get, if you shop at your local farmers markets; and ethnic food stores as well. Get to know them and see if they will work in your shopping routine.

Another good strategy is to buy your dry goods in bulk. You can really buy any foods that you are sure to eat before they go bad. Dry goods just tend to stay fresh longer (nonperishable).

Also, buying your foods when they are in season serves more than one purpose. You can save money on produce that is more readily available, and you can also benefit from getting the best tasting food because it is at its peak state of freshness.

Decide if any of these tips resonate with you, and help make your life easier. You really can save a surprising amount of money, when you put enough focused attention on it.

Chapter 7: The Way to Persevere

This chapter goes hand in hand with your driving force to achieve your goals. Persevering requires continuing on your intended path, even after it has been a while and it may not be easy. Sometimes a goal or change can be so clear and compelling that there is no question whether you can achieve it. However, after a period of time the reasons behind your motivation may be forgotten or may not have the same power they had before.

The key is to revive that original force. Make it as fresh as it was when you first made it. There are many ways to do this, and we will discuss some of them in this chapter. Keep an open mind as you read the tips I've provided, and see if any of them will work for you and your goals.

Sometimes it can take just one idea to set a spark; or to rekindle one. One great idea has the potential to push you through even the most difficult struggles. It can take you all the way through those struggles, towards your greatest achievements. And any obstacles you make it through builds your strength and determination. Losing your motivation can be a tragedy, when you know you have so much potential and unachieved goals. And sometimes you may even lose the progress you were building before you lost track. This can be such a shame. I have seen it happen to other people, and I have experienced it for myself. My goal is to prevent this for myself and to help others avoid it as well.

The first thing that I like to do when I lose motivation, for something I am working on, is to find that place where I was originally inspired. What made me create that goal or commitment in the first place? Was it something I saw or read? Did I speak with someone about it? Was it a thought I had, or state I was in? I find that I can at least spark my interest again if I take the right actions to remind myself. Just a little inspiration can go a long way toward retrieving your driving force.

Re-examine all of the work you did in chapter 2, in which we built up your WHY power. What are your reasons for wanting to achieve your goal? Are your reasons still valid for you? If not, discover some new reasons you want to achieve your goals. In thing case, why you want to improve your health, and adopt a plant based diet.

Another great way to rebuild your motivation is to see how far you have come. Look back to where you first started making changes. Have you made a lot of improvements? If so, be sure to applaud yourself for your progress. This will help you to see the value in doing what still needs to be accomplished.

Chapter 8: FAQ

Here are some of the most asked questions regarding the plant based diet. Hopefully this section will help to answer any questions that weren't answered for you in the rest of the main section of the book.

Which is better for you-a vegan or a vegetarian diet?

The answer to this really depends on your lifestyle and what you are trying to achieve. Also, you need to be aware of what you are willing to commit to. I personally do not eat dairy (due to an allergy), so not eating dairy is easier for me. So veganism is my diet of choice, but what you choose must be your own personal decision. Make it wisely!

Is yeast vegan?

Technically, mushrooms and yeast aren't "plants" since they belong to the Fungi kingdom, but these foods are eaten by vegans and people who follow a "plant-based diet". They are often included in the plant category- as are mushrooms.

Can you eat bread as a vegan?

Traditionally bread is made from yeast, flour and water, and so yes it is suitable for vegans, most of the time. Some commercially sold breads contain dairy or eggs so be sure to check ingredients before you purchase.

What is a minimally processed plant based food?

Minimally processed foods are tampered with only to a certain extent. This is mostly important because these kinds of foods can still maintain their nutritional value. Guacamole is an example of a plant food that is minimally processed or prepared.

Hummus, applesauce, salsa, peanut butter, oatmeal, and vegetable broth would be other examples.

Condiments such as mustard, hot sauce, vinegars, and soy sauce are also generally accepted as within the scope of "minimally processed".

Corn tortillas, whole-grain breads (e.g. whole-wheat bread), and pastas

How do vegans get enough protein?

There is really no need to worry about becoming deficient in protein if you are consuming enough calories to live. Humans cannot actually be deficient in protein unless they are starving. You can get all of the complete protein you need from plant sources.

Is it healthy for children to be on a vegan diet?

Yes, a vegan or vegetarian diet is a healthy part of an infant or child's life, as long as enough attention is paid to balance and wholesome plant based foods in the right amounts, but this is true with any regular diet.

How do I get enough calcium on a vegan diet? What about osteoporosis?

You will get plenty enough calcium with this eating, because you will be eating a lot of dark leafy greens, like broccoli and spinach; and from other plant sources like white beans, soy, almonds and rice. Also, you will get high amounts of all other life-building nutrients, as well. Exercise will also contribute to your prevention of osteoporosis.

Avoid calcium destroyers like tobacco, caffeine and excess salt.

What's wrong with drinking milk? Is organic milk better? Is soymilk a safer alternative? What about other dairy products?

Cow's milk is not the worst thing for you on the planet; but it is a rich source of cholesterol, saturated fat, and possibly added chemicals and hormones unless clearly stated.

Is it safe to eat soybeans and other soy foods?

Soy beans in their natural state are perfectly safe and healthy for you. Once you get into the more processed and packaged soy products, you run the risk of eating not-so-healthy vegetarian foods. Tofu should be fine, and is recommended. Edamame is an awesome protein-packed snack. And soymilk is processed to an extent, but a vast improvement from traditional cows' milk.

Are carbohydrates bad for you? Is it OK to eat carbohydrates if I am trying to lose weight?

Carbohydrates should not be labeled as an enemy, or as something you need to avoid, if you want to lose weight. Much of the country would probably want to lose weight if they knew they could. The key is to focus on whole plant based starches, and healthy grains. Whole grains, potatoes, whole wheat pasta, brown rice, and sweet potatoes. Avoid processed versions, which have lost much of their fiber and other nutrients.

Should I be on a gluten-free diet?

If you are experiencing any of the possible side effects of gluten intolerance, then a gluten-free diet would be beneficial to you. If you would like to see if eliminating gluten from your diet would make a positive difference in your health, then I would highly recommend it! You can try it out as a temporary experiment, and see how your body responds. Remember to always listen for your body's signals. There is a lot we don't know, that our body can tell us. Listen and learn.

Doesn't a vegetarian or vegan diet require a lot of planning and preparation?
Your diet is as easy of complicated as you want it to be. But I will say, and I believe many would agree with me, that proper planning and reparation will work beautifully in your favor in life. This is covered more in the section I have on meal planning.

CAN YOU GET FULL EATING ONLY PLANTS?
Yes, of course! Plants have a ton of fiber and protein, which fill you up the most. And they also provide you with the majority of your vital nutrients and vitamins. These foods will keep you fuller for longer; with less water retention and bloating as in traditional animal-based dishes.

Conclusion

I would like to thank you from the bottom of my heart, for reading my book. I really do appreciate it. The reason why I wanted to write this book is because I feel that there is a need for more quality information; that is available to anyone. I wanted to take all of the knowledge that I have learned about plant based diets, and share it where it is needed. Having the right information is key if you want to make the most informed decisions in your life. Unfortunately, in the health and diet industry there is plenty of misleading information, and it can be confusing and frustrating. Don't go for the quick fix. Stick to the most sustainable, logical, healthy habits. It is said that it takes somewhere between 3 weeks and one month to create a habit. So stick with it, and I am sure you will experience so many health benefits; you will be amazed at what you can accomplish. It is my deepest hopes that this book has been helpful to you. I hope that I have helped to bring you closer to the health you want to gain for yourself.

Part 2

Introduction

"The food you eat can be either the safest and most powerful form of medicine or the slowest form of poison." — Ann Wigmore

Congratulations on making this decision to improve your health and lifestyle by taking the first steps on your plant-based journey!

Whether you are new to this way of eating, would just like to dip your toes into a plant-based diet, change your eating habits, or are already a vegan and are looking into more options for food/recipes, this book is for you. I hope that you will gain the same benefits as I and many others have experienced following a plant-based diet.

Remember, I was in your shoes once upon a time too, and I know that changing the way you eat can seem intimidating. But the truth is, it's not about what you can't eat, it's about all the tasty, nutritious foods you can eat and how that food will nourish your body, mind, and mood.

This book is specifically focused on a plant-based diet, how to become a plant & veggie connoisseur, tips and tricks to help you along, and all the incredible benefits you can expect in the long run. If you're already a vegan, you can gain some new insights into foods and recipes you may not have tried yet.

My goal with this book is to inspire you to really want to give a plant-based diet a try, and to show you why you should. To give you this knowledge, you need to know how to transition healthily from eating meat, where to get your essential protein, calcium, and vitamins, how to structure your diet, and how to nourish your body properly.

Firstly, we need to note the difference between a vegan (veganism) and a plant-based diet. Veganism is a way of living that seeks to avoid (wherever possible) all forms of cruelty to animals for the purposes of producing food, clothing, cosmetics, or anything else.

A vegan diet eliminates all animal products, and vegans don't eat any food that's sourced from animals or any animal by-product (e.g., meat, milk, eggs, fish, or honey). It's not simply a case of a person "not eating meat"; it's a lifestyle and a specific way of thinking about animals. It's also important to point out that we are focusing on health, and a vegan lifestyle isn't necessarily a healthy one, it's a matter of how the individual vegan chooses to eat.

In recent years, plant-based diets have grown in popularity. But this type of diet can mean different things to different people.

A plant-based diet consists primarily or entirely of plants, including vegetables, grains, nuts, seeds, legumes, and fruits.

Most people see it as a 100% plant diet, while others include small quantities of animal products. Others consider it a vegan-style diet in which no animal products or animal by-products are allowed. We will be following this idea. All of the information and recipes in this book are built on the foundation of using absolutely no animal products whatsoever. That's why I can wholly recommend this book to vegans.

For the purposes of this book, I will frequently refer to 'plant-based food' as 'vegan food.' This is because many supermarkets/stores/restaurants will use the term 'vegan food' or just 'vegan' to refer to food and meals that contain no animal products. As this term is used so often, and you can expect to see it when you go grocery shopping, I will also use the term to avoid confusion.

Let's dive in.

According to a study conducted in 2017, at least 6% of people in the US identify as vegan, as opposed to 1% who did so in 2014. This is great news for finding vegan options when dining out and when shopping for groceries, as establishments will naturally want to cater to this growing trend.

Bear in mind that how you shape your plant-based diet is completely up to you. Foods such as fruits, vegetables, nuts, leafy greens, seeds, whole grains, and legumes are staples. However, you must aim for at least six servings of grains, five servings of nuts, legumes, and other protein sources like tofu, mushrooms, peanut butter, plant-based milk, and chickpeas.

You should also aim for at least four servings of veggies, two servings of healthy fats, and two servings of fruits. You don't even need to give up dessert. As somebody on a plant-based diet, let me tell you that the market is pretty great now for vegan ice cream, and there are even baked desserts with no eggs or butter. So, you can still indulge in a little treat now and then.

For so long, I hesitated to go plant-based - it was just too hard. I was always a meat & cheese lover. I grew up with meat dinners every single day. The more meat and cheese, the better. And I could never imagine being without it. When I tried to have a simple salad for lunch, I was starving - the veggies never filled me up! I tried for a day and gave up. I needed meat!

Me and food - it was a never-ending battle. I struggled with eating disorders, I tried all sorts of diets, fought a sugar addiction (yes, it's real), but in the end, I always went back to binging on candy and fast food - until it caught up with me.

I started to develop health problems. I was developing fungal infections in various parts of my body, particularly candidiasis, a form of fungal infection in the throat and gut.

These infections would flare up 4-6 times a year over many years, but eventually, they were showing up every single month for about two years. Every-single-month! You can imagine my desperation. I felt hopeless, and doctors didn't know what to do either.

Pills, creams, etc., would temporarily solve the problem, but the infection would soon be back the next month. I spent hundreds of hours researching causes online. I spoke to some nutritional advisors, tried many supplements, etc. After a few months, I found out - probably not surprisingly - that the cause was the food I ate and specifically, in my case, sugar.

What changed my life was a 21-day plant-based fast. I didn't eat any sugar, meat, milk, fast food, or anything of the sort - and that month, the infection stayed away! It was a breakthrough! And while I continued this "diet", especially no sugar, the infection never came back.

I believe what you put in your body; you will get back. Our body is like soil, and the food is the seed. If you feed your body fast food, sugar, and other bad things, you can't expect to get back fantastic health. You can get away with it for years and years, but it will come back to you one day.

One day you will reap what you sow. I just pray that the harvest will be vigorous health. And I'm here to help you on this journey. I have been through this, and if you are like me, if you love all the bad food that the world has to offer, if you are addicted to fast food and sugar, then you know how unbelievably hard it is to switch from bad to good food. Some people don't have this problem and will never understand that sugar addiction is real; they think you can only be addicted to drugs. But no, food is also a drug.

I try to apply the 80/20 rule - 80 % of food that is very healthy vs. 20% of food that is less healthy. I think we need a bit of balance when it comes to our diets. You have freedom, and you are the boss, just make the right choice. It's your everyday choices that matter.

So, I love cooking and love eating amazing plant-based food. But, I, sometimes, unfortunately, have to cook meat for my husband as I still haven't convinced him to go plant-based. I want to share those recipes with the world, share my knowledge, and also give hope to those who are as ill and maybe even as helpless as I once was. Over the years, I have seen so many people and read so many stories about sick people that were healed through a plant-based diet. They say that food is medicine and I absolutely agree.

Our body is our temple, and it's the only body we'll get. We should cherish it, and we should protect it, we should be kind to it, and feed it with good and nutritious food.

So, how do you get started on a plant-based diet?

Well, this book is full of information on how you can get started on a plant-based diet. This book will give you all the tips and tricks you'll need to set you off on your journey. It also has recipes and shopping lists to make your transition seamless. You will also learn how you can combat your cravings. Think of this beginner's guide as your "plant-based diet encyclopedia." The most important thing is not just to consume a plant-based diet, but to know how to stay healthy while on this type of diet.

When you're getting started on a plant-based diet, you don't necessarily have to go cold turkey right away. Start by preparing meat-free meals every week and then slowly substitute them with things like tofu, veggie burgers, and so on. If you are going plant-based just to lose weight, it is essential to exercise and consume fewer calories. Ensure that your meals have vegetables in them. This way, you get plenty of fiber and vitamins that will help you feel full for longer.

If you are choosing to go plant-based, I should point out that there is a slightly higher price tag to this diet. The vegetables, fruits, plant-based proteins, and wholegrain you need to fill your plate with are generally more costly compared to heavily processed foods like sugary cereals, bread, and candy. The good news is that this diet requires that you bypass the butcher, which helps a great deal in keeping the tabs reasonable.

Research shows that there is a really good chance that you will lose weight on a plant-based diet. This is because a plant-based diet generally means consuming fewer calories, thus helping you lose weight and achieve a lower body mass index (BMI). The trick with the plant-based diet is to do it right - eat lots of veggies, fruits, and whole grains. This will make you feel fuller with fewer calories each day, preventing you from eating too much. With this kind of calorie deficit and reasonable physical activity, you are bound to shed some weight.

How fast and whether you keep that weight off is up to you. A meta-analysis of over 90 studies demonstrated that lower levels of BMI, LDL-cholesterol, total cholesterol, and glucose levels were observed in vegans and vegetarians as opposed to people eating both meat and plants. An Italian study from 2017 linked vegan and vegetarian diets to lower risks of cancer and ischemic heart disease.

Another study involved 99 participants with type 2 diabetes following a vegan diet. After 22 weeks, vegans lost an average of 13 pounds vs. 9 in the ADA groups, based on findings reported in Diabetes Care (2006). In other words, if you are overweight, losing just 5-10% of your present weight goes a long way in staving off certain diseases.

That said, it is important that you consider the emotional aspects of becoming a plant-eater. If your family does not eat plant-based, and your child wants to, you should seek to understand why they are choosing this diet plan. While the reason may be perfectly fine and healthy, there are certain instances when children do it just so that they can lose weight. If you think that your child may have an eating disorder, seek medical advice immediately.

The truth is, being on a restrictive diet is challenging, especially for children who feel different from their peers. The last thing a child wants is to be excluded from eating experiences such as birthday parties, among others. This is what you must think about as parents and discuss as a family.

It is important that you and your children stick to the plant-based diet in all settings. This means that you must find strategies that will help to ensure that you have food to eat. Talk to them about dietary choices. Remember that eating is more than just filling the body with food. Eating should be fun, irrespective of what the diet is.

Chapter 1: Steps on How to Start a Plant-Based Diet

"Your health is what you make of it. Everything you do and think either adds to the vitality, energy, and spirit you possess or takes away from it."
- Ann Wigmore

One of the most beneficial things you will ever do for yourself and the rest of the world is transitioning to a plant-based diet. While this process can be intimidating at first, the truth is that it is easier than you might think.

I grew up in Central Europe, where regular meals were composed of things such as eggs, chicken, beef, dairy foods, and so many more animal products. Sad to say, but it's the truth.

I can't recall a single meal that didn't include one of these animal products - from childhood through teenagerhood to adulthood. You may have experienced similar.

The most important thing is to master the steps of transitioning into a plant-based diet. Trust me; when you fully transition into the plant-based lifestyle, you will be amazed at how life on this side is fuller and the grass greener.

You may be thinking, "but how can I do it?"

Here are some steps that will help make the transition seamless.

Step 1: Educate Yourself

Before you can transition into a plant-based diet with confidence, and increase your chances of success at it, you need to educate yourself on why you are considering it in the first place.

Are you doing it in the name of a fad?

Well, then you're on the wrong mission. However, when you learn the benefits of being on a plant-based diet, how to make it a lifestyle, and how other people out there have done it, you will be focused on making it work for you too. When you know why you're starting a plant-based diet in the first place, that will open your eyes, motivate you, and get you excited about it - all of which are key to achieving success and a healthy lifestyle.

Step 2: Crowd Out, Don't Cut Out

This is one of the most critical steps when transitioning to a plant-based diet. Think about it for a moment, if I told you to go grocery shopping but not to buy any meat, dairy products, or eggs, how would you feel? What would you say?

Chances are that you would feel like you're missing out, right?

However, if I were to flip the table and ask you to buy items such as kale, spinach, tomatoes, bananas, coconut milk, flax seeds, potatoes, berries, almonds, or mushrooms, you're not just being told exactly what to buy, you're hardly going to feel deprived, are you?

The truth is, when you approach a plant-based diet from the angle of crowding out animal products in favor of a whole heap of delicious and filling plant-based food options, everything becomes not only far easier, but far more fun. It's critical that you go for non-dairy kinds of milk, whole grains, veggies, fruits, seeds, nuts, and legumes to get started on your new plant-based diet. Try as much as you can to stay away from vegan replacement meats.

Step 3: Find Recipes for Inspiration

Growing up, I always thought that if there were no meat on my plate, I'd be left with nothing but a nibble of salad or steamed broccoli. Basically, rabbit food. I'm sure you've felt that way too.

The truth is that I just didn't realize how delicious and creative a plant-based diet could be. I started looking up simple vegan recipes online and found so much inspiration for creating a simple meal from readily available ingredients. This is how you set yourself up for success on a plant-based diet.

So, what are you waiting for?

Look out for simple recipe inspirations and try them out. The truth is that you will already have many of these ingredients in your pantry or fridge, and all you need is to shop for the right foods, embrace a new approach, and embrace a fresh lifestyle with zest and zeal.

Step 4: Go Out Shopping

Now that you have recipes for your plant-based diet, the next step is to go out shopping for the right vegan foods. The best thing is for you to buy all the vegan food you can get your hands on. Ensure that you stock up your pantry with as much produce as you possibly can - including healthy grains like wild rice, quinoa, and oats.

These foods are what form the foundation of your breakfast dishes, filling lunches, and satisfying dinners. It is important that you consider buying unsweetened almond milk instead of dairy milk too. Bring on the hemp, walnuts, chia, and flax seeds to get those healthy fats. Go for legumes such as green peas, lentils, chickpeas, and other types of beans.

The point is to try whole foods so that you can stay away from foods with added sugars as much as you can - to ensure that you have optimal blood sugar levels.

While shopping at the store, ensure that you pay attention to the ingredients on the label. The most important thing at this point is to embrace simple foods as much as possible. Don't forget to add in herbs and spices, as well as condiments - like tamari, stevia, balsamic vinegar, mustard, apple cider vinegar, and tahini. These are the things you need to add to your meals to make them taste more flavourful, decadent, and zesty!

Step 5: Focus on the Basics

Eating a plant-based diet does not have to be difficult. The best thing is for you to start with the basics when it comes to the first few meal batches.

For instance, for your breakfast, you can have oatmeal with cinnamon, almond milk, coconut yogurt, and chopped fruit. For lunch, you can have soup and salad. The good thing with these meals is that you can prepare them beforehand and stock them up in the fridge so that you can grab them on the go. For dinner, you can have some pan-fried roasted veggies with seasoning. You can accompany that with mushrooms, kale, quinoa, and garlic.

Remember, basic ingredients taste best. You don't need to go all fancy unless you want to. When you are in doubt, turn to a smoothie to spice things up. The truth is that smoothies are the perfect way of filling the gaps, making things creative, and makings things delicious.

Step 6: Take One Day at a Time

When you are learning to transition to a plant-based diet, you must learn not to overwhelm yourself. You don't have to make your meals complicated or cook them in a gourmet style. The trick is to take everything easy and count each day as it comes.

With time, you will realize that your meals get better. So, don't beat yourself up, stress over it, or feel intimidated by a plant-based diet. This is a diet like any other, and you have to allow yourself time to ease in. The simpler you keep your meals, the better things will be for you.

Step 7: Eat Whole Foods as Much as You Can

It's quite easy to go plant-based and end up eating processed vegan foods. However, that's not the best way to go about a plant-based diet. Instead of going all-in with processed vegan foods, the way better option is to buy whole foods as much as you can to ensure that your diet is balanced and that you are consuming the right balance of foods. This way, you get sufficient nutrition, and you are satisfied after every meal.

You don't have to abandon your coconut ice cream or dark chocolate completely. You can indulge in your favorites once in a while - just not all the time.

With a plant-based diet, you won't just enjoy its health benefits, but also appreciate the Earth and its animals animals, and create a stronger connection with yourself and the people around you. You will also enjoy better hair, sleep, skin, digestion, and nails. Outside of your plant-based diet, you must supplement with vitamin B12, D, and energy by taking multivitamins, probiotics, and anything else that will offer you nutritional support.

How then can you save time and money on a plant-based diet?

Plan meals in advance

One of the best ways to save money at the grocery store is to sit down each weekend and plan your meals for the week. Make a list of what you will eat each day. When planning your meals, check your refrigerator for any perishables you need to consume soon and incorporate them into your recipes.

To save more time, you can double some dinner recipes to use for lunch or leftovers later in the week.

Make a shopping list

If you use a shopping list every time you go to the store, you're far more likely to avoid making impulse buys, which can save money. Before making your shopping list, be sure you also check the pantry or cupboards to see what you may need to replenish. Then, using your meal plan, make a list of the ingredients you need.

You can further increase your savings by shopping based on store specials. Many grocery stores now have saving cards for tablets, smartphones, or computers that allow you to view real-time store circulars and download coupons to your device. If you prefer a lower-tech option, you can also clip coupons and use store ads that come in the mail or newspaper. Using these tools as you plan meals is an excellent way to save money.

Shop wise and healthy

Setting up your vegan pantry is relatively straightforward. Every ingredient should be nutrient-dense. Certain packaged foods such as cereals, orange juice, and vegan milk can boost your intake of nutrients as they are fortified with essential vitamins and minerals.

Many of these ingredients are available in bulk at your local supermarket, so you may want to invest in a few airtight containers to store unpackaged or loosely packaged foods.

It's also a good idea to start a collection bin for food scraps, as almost all vegetable peelings and excess cuttings can be used to make vegetable stock.

Vacuum-sealed packages of vegan milk are becoming widely available. Vegan sour cream, usually derived from soy, is similar in texture and taste to cow-milk sour cream.

Chapter 2: Foods Healthy Vegans Eat

"You have only one body, you will not get another one, so take care of it." - Author Unknow

∞∞∞

As we have already discussed, vegans avoid animal-sourced products. They do this either for the sake of the environment, their health, or for ethical reasons.

Unfortunately, sticking to a plant-based diet puts several people at a higher risk of nutritional deficiencies. This especially happens when plant-based diets are not well-planned.

If you're a vegan or starting a plant-based diet and would like to stay healthy, it's important that you ensure you're consuming nutrient-rich foods that are whole and fortified. Here are some of the foods you must consider in your diet plan.

Legumes

As you try to eat fewer animal products, shed a few pounds, and get healthy, you must avoid traditional sources of protein like eggs, poultry, meat, and fish. But the big question is how to replace this protein with plant-based products. Well, the first food that you can use as an alternative source of protein is legumes. These include beans, peas, and lentils. These contain at least 10-20 grams of protein per cooked cup.

The good thing about legumes is that they're an excellent source of slowly digested carbs, fiber, folate, iron, zinc, manganese, antioxidants, and other health-promoting compounds. That said, bear in mind that legumes have a good amount of anti-nutrients that lower the body's ability to absorb minerals.

For example, research shows that iron absorption from plants is approximately 50% lower than that of animal sources. A vegetarian diet has been shown to have reduced zinc absorption by about 35% compared to diets containing meat. This explains why most people prefer sprouting, fermenting, or cooking their legumes because, in so doing, they lower the levels of anti-nutrients.

To increase the absorption of zinc and iron from legumes, don't go overboard on their consumption as much as you can, ditto for calcium-rich foods. This is because calcium has been shown to hinder absorption if consumed at the same time. When you consume legumes in combination with vitamin C-rich veggies and fruits, this further increases the absorption of iron.

The bottom line here is, legumes, such as beans, peas, and lentils, serve as alternative sources of animal-derived foods that fit in your vegan diet. To increase the absorption of nutrients, it is important that you ferment, sprout, or cook your legumes well.

Nuts, seeds, and nut butter

One of the other great additions to the plant-based diet is the consumption of nuts, nut butter, and seeds. This is in part because an ounce serving of nuts or seeds contains about 5-12 grams of protein. This makes them excellent alternatives to protein-rich foods derived from animals.

Additionally, nuts, seeds, and nut butter are loaded with minerals like selenium, zinc, fiber, magnesium, Vitamin E, and iron. They also contain high quantities of antioxidants and other plant-based compounds that are beneficial to the human body.

Nuts are versatile. You can consume them alone or add them to interesting recipes like desserts, sauces, and cheeses. One of the most delicious options I love is cashew cheese. The trick is for you to choose unblanched or unroasted varieties as much as possible, considering that nutrients can be lost during processing.

Go for nuts that are natural as opposed to ones that are heavily processed - mainly because they are devoid of oil, salt, and sugars that are added to household varieties.

The bottom line here is that nuts, nut butter, and seeds are nutritious, rich in protein and nutrients, and are quite versatile. Ensure that they are not missing from your pantry!

Flax, hemp, and chia seeds

These three types of seeds contain a distinctive profile of nutrients that deserve to be highlighted. All these seeds are packed with large quantities of protein that other seeds simply do not have.

For instance, an ounce of hemp seeds contains at least 9 grams of complete and easily digestible protein. This translates to at least 50% more protein vs. other types of seeds. They are also loaded with omega-3 and omega-6 fatty acids. According to research, the fats found in hemp seeds are effective at reducing the symptoms of PMS (Postmenstrual Syndrome) and menopause.

These seeds have also been reported to reduce inflammations and improve skin conditions.

Flaxseeds and chia seeds are loaded with large quantities of alpha-linoleic acid (ALA), which is an essential omega-3 fatty acid the body can comfortably convert into EPA and DHA.

EPA and DHA play essential roles in the development and maintenance of the nervous system. They are long-chain fatty acids that play a significant part in alleviating depression, pain, anxiety, and inflammation. Considering that EPA and DHA are primarily found in fish and seaweed, the truth is that it is challenging for vegans to get enough of this in their diet. This is why you must consider consuming ALA-rich foods like flaxseeds and chia seeds.

That said, research shows that the body has the ability to convert at least 0.5-5% of ALA to form DHA and EPA. Irrespective of this, the truth is that chia seeds and flaxseeds are very healthy and make a great substitute for eggs in baking. The bottom line here is that seeds like hemp, chia, and flax are loaded with proteins and ALA compared to other seeds, and you must include them in your diet.

Tofu and other minimally processed meat alternatives

Did you know that tofu and tempeh are minimally processed meat substitutes made from soybeans?

Now you know!

One thing to note is that tofu and tempeh are loaded with at least 16-19 grams of protein per 3-and-a-half-ounce portions. They are good sources of calcium and iron. Tofu is made by pressing soybean curds and is a popular meat replacement. To prepare it, you can sautée, grill or scramble it. It also serves as a great alternative to eggs in recipes like quiches, omelets, and frittatas.

Tempeh, on the other hand, is produced by fermenting soybeans. It has a distinct flavor that makes it a popular replacement for fish. However, you can also use tempeh in several other dishes. The process of fermentation plays a significant role in lowering the number of anti-nutrients that naturally occur in soybeans. This may increase the number of nutrients the body can absorb from tempeh.

Additionally, the process of fermenting tempeh produces small quantities of Vitamin B12, a nutrient found in animal foods and which soybean does not typically contain. However, what is still unclear is whether the type of Vitamin B12 found in tempeh is active in humans. It is also important to note that the quantity of Vitamin B12 in tempeh is low and varies from one brand to the other. This means that as a vegan, you can't rely fully on tempeh as a source of this vitamin.

Another popular meat alternative is seitan, which offers about 25 grams of wheat protein per 100 grams. This meat alternative also serves as a good source of selenium along with trace amounts of calcium, iron, and phosphorus.

However, if you have celiac disease or gluten sensitivity, you should avoid seitan because of the high gluten content. The bottom line here is that minimally processed meat alternatives - such as tempeh, tofu, and seitan - are nutrient-rich additions to your plant-based diet. It is important that you limit your consumption of heavily processed vegan mock meats to ensure that you stay healthy, however.

Calcium-fortified plant milk and yogurt

One thing you might notice about vegans is that they tend to consume smaller quantities of calcium per day compared to vegetarians and meat-eaters. This affects their overall bone health - especially when calcium intake is below 525 mg per day. Because of this, you must consider upping your calcium consumption via plant milk and yogurt.

If you are looking to increase your protein intake as a vegan, opt for milk and yogurt derived from hemp and soy. Other alternatives that are lower in protein include coconut, rice, almond, and oat milk.

The good thing about calcium-fortified milk and yogurt is that they are rich in Vitamin D, a nutrient responsible for the absorption of calcium. That said, other brands add Vitamin B12 into their products. This means that for you to reach the recommended daily intake of calcium, Vitamin B12, and D, you must go for fortified products. You can choose the unsweetened options to limit your sugar intake.

The bottom line here is that plant milk and yogurt fortified with vitamin B12, D, and calcium serve as good alternative products to the cow milk other people are used to.

Seaweed

This is one of the rare plants that is loaded with high quantities of DHA, an essential fatty acid with several health benefits. Other good sources of protein in this category include algae like Chlorella and spirulina.

When you take two tablespoons of seaweed, you ingest about 8 grams of protein.

It is important to note that seaweed contains minerals such as manganese, magnesium, potassium, riboflavin, iodine, and high quantities of antioxidants. In particular, iodine plays a significant role in promoting the metabolism and function of the thyroid gland. Iodine's RDI is estimated at 150 micrograms/day. To meet your dietary requirement of iodine, you need to consume at least several servings of seaweed every week.

That said, there are certain types of seaweed - such as kelp - that are known to contain extremely high quantities of iodine. This means that you need to avoid eating them in large amounts. However, certain varieties like spirulina contain only small amounts of iodine.

If you have difficulty meeting your recommended daily intake through seaweed alone, aim to consume at least 2.5 ml of iodized salt every day. Just like tempeh, seaweed is promoted as a good source of Vitamin B12 for vegans.

While it contains a form of Vitamin B12, the truth is that it is not clear whether this form is active in humans or not.

The bottom line here is that seaweed is rich in protein and serves as a good source of fatty acids. It is also loaded with iodine and antioxidants. However, they should not be relied upon as your sole source of Vitamin B12.

Nutritional yeast

This is made from deactivated Saccharomyces cerevisiae yeast. It is often found in the form of yellow powder or flakes in health food stores and supermarkets. An ounce of nutritional yeast contains at least 7 grams of fiber and 14 grams of protein. They are also commonly fortified with minerals such as magnesium, manganese, zinc, copper, and B vitamins, including B12.

This means that fortified nutritional yeast is a practical way for vegans to achieve their daily recommended requirement of Vitamin B12. That said, Vitamin B12 is light-sensitive and is likely to degrade if stored in a clear plastic bag. Non-fortified nutritional yeast, on the other hand, should not be depended upon as your sole source of Vitamin B12.

The bottom line here is that fortified nutritional yeast is rich in protein and serves as a source of Vitamin B12. However, you shouldn't rely on it as your sole source of vitamins.

Sprouted and fermented plant foods

Even though they are loaded with nutrients, the truth is that most plants contain different quantities of antinutrients. These antinutrients often lower the body's ability to absorb the minerals contained in these foods.

Sprouting and fermenting are considered to be some of the most straightforward and time-tested techniques of lowering the anti-nutrients present in various foods. These methods increase the quantities of beneficial nutrients absorbed from plant foods and can boost protein quality. Interestingly, sprouting has been shown to slightly lower the amount of gluten in certain cereals.

Fermented plants, on the other hand, serve as good sources of probiotic bacteria that play a significant role in boosting digestive health and immune function. They are also thought to contain Vitamin K2, which promotes bone and dental health. This vitamin also lowers the risk of developing heart disease and certain cancers.

The best trick is to try fermenting or sprouting some of these grains at home. If you don't want to do this at home, you can walk to your local store and buy some that have already been fermented or sprouted for you. These include miso, tempeh, pickles, natto, kombucha, sauerkraut, and kimchi.

The bottom line here is that the sprouting and fermenting of foods play a significant role in enhancing their nutritional value, fermented foods, for instance, offer vegans the perfect source of probiotics and Vitamin K2.

Whole grains, pseudocereals, and cereals

Cereals, pseudocereals, and whole grains are a perfect source of complex carbs, iron, fiber, and other B vitamins. They are also packed with minerals such as zinc, magnesium, selenium, and phosphorus.

That said, certain varieties are more nutritious than others - especially when it comes to protein.

For example, teff and spelt contain at least 10-11 grams of protein/cup. This is way than wheat and rice. Pseudocereals come in second - such as amaranth and quinoa - with about 9 grams of protein/cooked cup. These are also the two rarest sources of complete protein in this food group.

Just like several other plant foods, it is important to note that whole grains and pseudocereals are packed with varying levels of anti-nutrients that limit the absorption of beneficial nutrients. However, if you sprout them, you lower the levels of these anti-nutrients significantly.

The bottom line here is that teff, spelt, quinoa, and amaranth are high protein substitutes compared to better-known grains like rice and wheat. However, when you sprout them, you get the optimal protein sources.

Choline-rich foods

Nutrients such as choline play a significant role in improving the health of the liver, nervous system, and the brain. The truth is that the human body can produce choline, though only in small quantities. This explains why it is considered an essential nutrient in your diet.

Choline is found in small quantities in a wide range of fruits, legumes, nuts, grains, and vegetables. Certain plant foods - such as tofu, cauliflower, quinoa, soymilk, and broccoli - have the most substantial amounts of choline.

During pregnancy, a woman's daily choline requirements increase significantly. Additionally, heavy drinkers, endurance athletes, and postmenopausal women are said to be at a higher risk of developing choline deficiency. So, if you fall into one of these categories, you need to make a special effort to ensure that you have sufficient choline-rich foods on your plate.

The bottom line is that choline-rich foods - like cauliflower, soy, quinoa, and broccoli - should be included in a vegan diet to ensure better wellbeing of the body.

Vegetables and fruits

Did you know that there are certain vegans who rely heavily on mock meats and vegan junk foods to replace their favorite animal foods? Are you one of them?

The truth is that these types of foods are highly processed and not healthy for you at all. You need to look for healthy, natural substitutes. That is fruits and vegetables that are packed with vitamins and minerals.

For example, you can use mashed bananas to substitute eggs in your baking recipes. Another popular replacement is banana ice cream to substitute dairy-based ice cream. All you need to do is blend a few frozen bananas until you get a smooth paste. Then you just need to add your favorite toppings. On the other hand, mushrooms - such as Portobello and cremini – as well as eggplants, are a great way to get that meaty texture without the actual meat. Mushrooms are also great for grilling. You can also consume jackfruit as a stand-in for meat in savory dishes like barbecue sandwiches and stir-fries. You can also use cauliflower as a versatile addition to a number of recipes, like pizza crusts.

You should also increase your daily intake of iron and calcium in fruits and veggies. These foods include leafy greens, like spinach, bok choy, watercress, kale, and mustard greens. Other great options are artichokes, broccoli, blackcurrants, and turnip greens, among others.

The bottom line here is that fruits and veggies are healthy options you can consume as alternatives to animal foods.

So, what is the take-home message here?

Well, we already know that vegans avoid all foods derived from animal sources such as meat and dairy products. This can limit the intake of certain nutrients while increasing the dietary requirements of others.

If you plan your plant-based diet to include sufficient amounts of the foods we have already discussed in this chapter, you will not only stay healthy but also avoid any nutrient deficiencies. Nonetheless, there are vegans who find it hard to consume foods that cover all their nutrient needs. If that is the case for you, you can supplement it with a good back-up option.

Chapter 3: Plant-Based Nutrition Guide

"Life is as dear to a mute creature as it is to man. Just as one wants happiness and fears pain, just as one wants to live and not die, so do other creatures."- The Dalai Lama

If you are truly planning to eat a vegan diet, it is crucial that you master the basics of vegan nutrition. The main pitfalls of a vegan diet are quite simple to avoid once you know what nutrients you need.

When you choose to go plant-based, or are moving in that direction, you are setting yourself up for huge health benefits. A diet that is built primarily on plants is linked to lower levels of cholesterol and a reduced risk of developing type 2 diabetes.

Additionally, plant-based foods are loaded with compounds that have anti-cancer properties. Also, many people find that replacing eggs, dairy, and meat with foods loaded with fiber gets them closer to a healthier weight.

When you eat a variety of whole plant foods along with other foods loaded with healthy fats, you increase your chances of warding off chronic diseases. However, when you are on a plant-based diet, you require a little additional attention to ensure that you're fulfilling your nutrient needs. This chapter aims to discuss the essential things you must keep in mind to ensure that you have adequate nutrition when you are on a plant-based diet.

Nothing we present here should be challenging to understand. Heading towards a plant-based diet simply means finding a whole new way of meeting your nutrient needs. Once you master the basics of proper meal planning, adhering to this diet becomes second nature.

So, what are your nutrient recommendations for a plant-based diet?

Well, it doesn't matter whether you're already vegan or not. The most important thing on this journey is to ensure that you're loading up your basket and plate with a wide range of veggies, beans, seeds, nuts, and whole grains.

Even after you've made these healthy choices as the foundation of your diet, it is entirely possible to come up short on one or more of these important nutrients.

That said, some of the nutrients you must focus on more when you're on a plant-based diet include protein, iron, calcium, zinc, Vitamin B12, omega-3, iodine, and Vitamin D.

As we have already mentioned, a Western diet typically derives these from animal products. However, when you are a vegan, you don't have to worry, considering that you get all the above nutrients in plant-based foods - except B12 and D vitamins. Here, we will discuss how you can supplement these in your diet too.

Protein

According to several studies, it's no secret that vegans do not suffer a severe risk of protein deficiency as long as they load up their diet with enough calories and consume whole plant foods, although this isn't as simple as it seems. In as much as we don't see vegans with overt protein deficiency, that does not necessarily mean that every vegan consumes the optimum amount of protein.

One thing you must bear in mind is that marginal or suboptimal protein status is damaging to one's overall health - it affects muscle strength and bone health. This explains why it is especially important to incorporate legumes in your diet so that you have an adequate quantity of amino acids - the building blocks of protein. A vegan diet that doesn't include legumes risks falling short of certain essential amino acids, like lysine.

When you consume two servings a day of legumes, you will get a sufficient amount of lysine. However, adding an extra serving - to make it a total of three - adds an extra layer of safety. If you are advanced in age or are working on losing weight, it is in your interest to get more of these foods on your plate every day.

How then can you ensure that you eat protein-rich legumes?

While 2-3 servings of legumes a day may sound a lot, the truth is that the serving portions of these foods are surprisingly small. The following count as a serving of legumes - you can pick any of these.

- **¼ cup peanuts or soy nuts**

- ½ cup cooked dried beans or lentils
- 2 tbsps. of peanut butter
- 3 oz. veggie meat
- ½ cup tofu or tempeh
- 1 cup of soy milk or milk made from pea protein

Tip: This does not include other kinds of plant milk, as most of them are too low in protein composition.

Even though a lot of the foods on a plant-based diet might be new to your diet, increasing your legume intake is quite easy. Some of the foods you can integrate into your plant-based diet that include legumes are scrambled tofu, veggie burgers, lentil soup, bean burritos, peanut butter and jelly sandwiches, cereal with soy milk, veggies with peanut sauce, tacos with veggie ground beef, tossed salads topped with soy nuts, and hummus wraps, among others.

Iron and zinc

Whole grains and beans are loaded with iron, and a range of other vegan foods have minerals in them. However, what most people don't get is that many plant foods have certain compounds within, referred to as phytates, which bind iron, thus inhibiting their absorption. Luckily enough, it's quite easy to counter the effects of phytates on iron absorption. For instance, when you toast seeds and nuts, you make the iron in them readily available.

That said, one of the most effective ways to make iron available is the consumption of Vitamin C. When this is consumed at the same time as iron-rich foods, it helps to break the bond between iron and phytate, thus significantly increasing its absorption.

On a plant-based diet, one of the ways you can meet your iron needs is to consume plenty of beans, leafy greens, whole and enriched grains, and dried fruits, among others.

It is also important that as you consume these foods, you add in Vitamin C- rich foods along with them. Some rich sources of Vitamin C include citrus fruits and juices, mango, cantaloupe, strawberries, kiwifruit, broccoli, cabbage, papaya, peppers, pineapple, brussels sprouts, cauliflower, and tomato juice, among others.

Some of the best sources of zinc in plant-based diets include legumes, seeds, whole grains, and nuts. Just like iron, zinc is also bound to phytates, which, in turn, lower their absorption. In this case, the intake of Vitamin C will not help increase zinc absorption. However, certain food preparation practices make the zinc in your foods readily available for ease of absorption. For instance, when you add yeast or sourdough to whole grain bread, you make the zinc more absorbable. This simply means that whole grain breads are better sources of zinc compared to flatbreads, crackers, or cooked grains.

Sprouting grains and legumes have also been shown to increase zinc absorption.

Vitamin A

Plant-based foods do not really contain Vitamin A. However, fruits and veggies are loaded with precursors that the body converts to Vitamin A molecules. Some of these precursors include beta-carotene, which is found abundantly in dark leafy veggies like spinach and kale. They are also found in orange veggies like sweet potatoes, winter squash, and carrots, among others.

Having at least 1-2 servings of these veggies will go a long way in taking care of your Vitamin-A needs. You can also drizzle a little bit of oil over your veggies or dressing of avocado or tahini in your food to increase the ability of the body to absorb Vitamin A.

Omega-3 fatty acids

This is one of the nutrients that often eludes vegans who otherwise consume healthy fatty acids, referred to as alpha-linolenic acid (ALA). The truth is, omega-3 fatty acids are only found in a handful of plant foods. To ensure that you meet your dietary requirements, it is important that you add one or more of the following into your daily plant-based diet:

- 1 ½ tsp. hemp seed oil

- 1 tbsp. walnut or canola oil

- 1 ½ tsp. chia seeds

- 1 tbsp ground flaxseed

- ½ tbsp. hemp seeds

- ½ tbsp. chopped walnuts

- 1½ tbsp. flaxseed oil

Tip: Ensure that the flaxseeds you are adding into your diet are ground. Otherwise, you risk not absorbing ALA.

Even though the list of plant foods that absorb ALA is pretty short, it isn't difficult to get your daily requirement. It's as simple as stirring a handful of chia seeds into your cereal or adding a tablespoon of flaxseeds in quinoa or rice at dinner.

Dha and Epa

These two are different variants of omega-3 fats. They are not really considered dietary components considering that the body can synthesize them. However, the body can only do that if it gets the required ALA. One thing you must realize is that the conversion of these fats is often inefficient, and according to research, vegans have been shown to have low blood levels of EPA and DHA.

How much does this matter?

Well, it's not exactly clear!

More research reveals conflicting results as to whether these nutrients improve cognitive function and heart health. Some experts speculate that when there is insufficient intake of DHA and EPA, there is a risk of canceling out certain heart-health benefits. Additionally, some research indicates that EPA plays a significant role in alleviating depression.

Even though most people get these nutrients from fatty fish or fish oil supplements, the truth is that many companies sell vegan versions of these supplements - most of which are derived from microalgae, the same place fish source their omega-3 fats.

That said, don't hesitate to include other fat-rich foods into your plant-based diet. According to current health recommendations, the correct fat intake for good health lies anywhere between 20-35 % of your daily calories. This simply translates to between 22 and 39 grams of fat per every 1,000 calories you consume.

What matters is not really how much fat you consume at the end of the day. Instead, it's the type of fat you choose to ingest that truly matters. Unsaturated fats derived from plant sources contain healthy cholesterol levels, which, in turn, help lower the risk of heart health.

Additionally, specific plant-foods that are rich in fats are thought to offer unique health benefits unrelated to their fat content. For instance, tree nuts like cashews, almonds, pecans, and walnuts are said to lower the risk of heart disease. Certain soy foods with a higher fat content than legumes are loaded with a compound referred to as isoflavone - a phytoestrogen that lowers the risk of cancer while boosting artery health significantly. Extra virgin olive oil, on the other hand, is thought to serve as a good source of certain compounds that have anti-inflammatory properties.

Along with their health benefits, certain fat-rich foods play a significant role in helping vegans meet specific nutrient needs. Seeds, for instance, are good sources of zinc, and avocados are packed with Vitamin E, which has antioxidant properties.

Calcium

According to early research, vegans are said to require less calcium in their diet compared to omnivores. The theory that underlies this is that animal protein causes bones to lose calcium, thus creating a deficiency, especially for those who consume eggs, meat, and milk. With the evolution of research, it is clearer that protein plays a significant role in protecting bone health, and the amount of protein you eat does not affect your calcium needs.

While it is essential to consume adequate amounts of calcium, the most important thing is to focus on how this mineral is absorbed - something that differs from one food to the other. For instance, spinach - which is rich in calcium - has its calcium bound to oxalates, which block the body from absorbing it. On the other hand, swiss chard and beet greens contain substantial quantities of oxalates. In contrast, the absorption of calcium from certain veggies in the cabbage family - such as broccoli, bok choy, kales, and turnip greens - is said to be excellent.

Calcium is well-absorbed from certain fortified kinds of plant milk and tofu - made with calcium sulfate. However, you must be careful when buying your tofu, because unless it lists calcium sulfate in its ingredients, the calcium content is insignificant. That said, tahini, beans, and almonds contain moderate amounts of calcium that are not well-absorbed.

How then can you meet your daily calcium requirement in your plant-based diet?

Well, one rule of thumb for getting adequate amounts of calcium in your plant-based diet is to consume at least three cups of plant-foods loaded with calcium every day. Some options include tofu with calcium sulfate, cooked Chinese cabbages, mustard greens, collards, turnip greens, broccoli, kales, and bok choy, among others. You can also get this from certain types of plant milk and juices that are fortified with calcium.

The next thing is for you to aim at consuming at least three servings of other food with moderate quantities of calcium - such as okra, almonds, beans, kale, navel oranges, blackstrap molasses, figs, sweet potatoes, and corn tortillas, among others.

If you're over 50 years old, then it is advisable that you bump up your calcium intake by filling your plate with calcium-rich foods - an additional cup will do. As you advance in age, you become less efficient in absorbing calcium. This means that you will need to increase your dietary calcium intake slightly more than usual. Failure to consume calcium-rich foods regularly increases the risk of certain diseases, like osteoporosis.

Vitamin B12

There is so much information online that is misleading about Vitamin B12. To be specific, certain websites and forums claim that vegans don't need to worry about their B12. However, nutrition experts agree that there are two main sources of Vitamin B12 for vegans. These include foods that are fortified with this nutrient and B12 supplements.

Contrary to this belief, fermented foods, sea veggies, and organic veggies do not contain Vitamin B12. While nutritional yeast contains B12, the only way it can contain this nutrient is if it is grown in an environment that is loaded with this nutrient in the first place. Yes, people store significant quantities of B12 in their liver, but this does not mean that it is a reliable source of this vitamin.

Recommendations for Vitamin B12 supplements

When you start your plant-based dietary journey, the first thing you need to do is start taking B12 supplements. The truth is that there is no reason not to start immediately. One thing you must bear in mind is that when you are deficient in this nutrient, you are setting yourself up for anemia - which leads to nerve damage, something that, in most cases, is irreversible. This is why you must start taking B12 supplements immediately.

Determining the right dose is quite tricky, considering the fact that absorption varies based on the size of the dose. According to research, this nutrient is absorbed best in small quantities, hence the reason why you should take it in little doses. This also means that you need this nutrient in more copious amounts so that you lower the number of times you take it.

Some of the recommended ways to meet this dietary requirement include;

- Taking a daily dose of 25-100 mcg of Vitamin B12. Take it better by opting for a chewable to allow for greater absorption.

- Taking a supplement that offers at least 1000 mcg of vitamin B12 twice a week.

- Consuming at least two servings daily of plant-based food that is fortified with Vitamin B12 – with at least 2.5-3.5 mcg each of this nutrient. It is important that you eat these foods at least 4 hours apart to ensure optimal absorption.

That said, all these refer to cyanocobalamin as the form of vitamin considered to be the only reliable supplement.

Vitamin D

Humans have evolved to make Vitamin D, especially during summer, when sunlight hits your bare skin. However, we wear sunscreen, the clouds and smog cover the sunlight, and all these block the synthesis of this nutrient. According to research, older people and those with dark skin need more exposure to the sun for them to make Vitamin D. On the other hand, for those who live in temperate climates, the winter sunlight is often too weak for them to synthesize adequate Vitamin D.

It is important that you expose your face and arms to summer sunlight for at least 30 minutes every day without wearing sunscreen. If you are above 70 years of age, over 30 minutes of sunlight exposure every day should allow you to generate adequate amounts of Vitamin D. But what if you are not able to get this sunlight exposure every day? Well, in that case, you need it from your dietary sources.

There are several sources of Vitamin D, most of which are not vegan-friendly. For instance, this nutrient is naturally occurring in eggs and certain types of fish - though in small quantities. This simply means that everyone, whether vegan or not, must take Vitamin D supplements every day and eat fortified foods to ensure that they are not deficient.

The most common type of Vitamin D is D3, found in supplements and foods, and is almost always derived from animals. Vitamin D2, on the other hand, is derived from yeast, and until recently, it was the only form of this type of vitamin for vegans. If you have sufficient levels of vitamins, D2 supplements are enough to maintain these levels.

That said, research has demonstrated that D3 is effective at reversing a deficiency of Vitamin D. Therefore, if your levels are currently too low, D3 will bring it back up. Even though finding D3 for a vegan is quite hard, the truth is that vegan D3 supplements are now available, and the recommended intake is about 600 IUs/day.

Iodine

For a healthy thyroid gland, your body needs iodine. Even though plant-foods provide iodine, its specific quantities depend on where the food was grown.

Most people derive their iodine from dairy products and iodized salts. The iodine people get from cow milk comes primarily from cleaning solutions applied to the milking equipment and udders. But this is not for you as a vegan.

Sea vegetables are loaded with iodine, but their levels vary considerably. There are seaweeds that contain excessive quantities of iodine and so must be consumed in moderation. A small amount of iodine from iodized salts a day or 75 micrograms of iodine supplements at least 3-4 times/week go a long way in ensuring that you meet your dietary requirements.

Simple guidelines for plant-based nutrition

While wading through all these details, did you feel overwhelmed?

Well, don't give up!

The truth is that you can substantially improve your diet by developing certain habits that are easy to learn. All these guidelines will help compact the information we have discussed above into simple steps that will ensure that your plant-based diet is not only healthy but also well-balanced.

First, eat at least three servings a day of tofu, beans, soy milk, tempeh, peanuts, veggie meats, or peanut butter. Second, you must consume a wide range of vegetables and fruits. This should include leafy greens and dark orange vegetables. Mix this with a good source of Vitamin C, such as citrus fruits, peppers, or strawberries.

Third, ensure that you get most of your fats from healthy plant sources such as nuts, seeds, avocados, and moderate quantities of oils. Ensure that you also load up on essential omega-3 fat ALA from sources like walnuts, flaxseeds, canola oil, and hempseed.

Fourth, ensure that you eat at least three cups of calcium-rich foods each day. This should include fortified plant-based milk, tofu with calcium sulfate in it, fortified juices, bok choy, cooked kales, turnip greens, and collards. If you like eating raw greens instead of cooked, double the number of greens.

Fifth, try as much as you can to take your supplements. The truth is that you need Vitamin B12 supplements or fortified foods. You also need Vitamin D supplements, especially during the winter months. You may also wish to consider taking DHA and EPA supplements. If you also don't use iodized salts regularly, consider taking an iodine supplement.

That said, avoid needless dietary restrictions. When you place unnecessary dietary restrictions on your food choices, you can make it harder to meet all your nutritional needs. You will also make it harder for yourself to stick to a plant-based diet. The truth is, restrictive versions of the plant-based diet - such as raw foods or very low-fat - do not have an advantage over those diets that include higher fats and cooked foods.

Yes, it is smart to eat plenty of fruits, veggies, whole grains, and legumes, but the truth is that you have no reason to avoid vegan meats, oils, and plant-based milk. Realize that these foods not only make your plant-based diet tasty and convenient, but they also contribute plenty of essential nutrients. There is no evidence that vegans who avoid these foods enjoy better health than the rest of us.

If you follow these guidelines, you'll not only meet your plant-based nutritional requirements, but you'll also have an edge against diabetes, heart disease, high blood pressure, and certain cancers. Of course, there is no guarantee that a diet can totally prevent any illness, but when you pay attention to the guidance we have discussed here, you will be more confident about laying a solid foundation for incredible long-term health.

The bottom line is, with a well-planned plant-based diet, you can adequately fulfill your nutritional needs.

Chapter 4: Preparing for Success

The five commandments of a good plant-based diet:

Commandment #1 Avoid refined white flour

White flour is heavily processed and bleached. Your white flour lacks germ, bran, iron, and B vitamins. Think of it as an empty nutritional shell with nothing inside. According to research, this kind of flour can cause bloating, and when it is mixed with sugar, it potentially leads to weight gain, type 2 diabetes, and insulin resistance.

As you may already know, this kind of flour is used in pasta, bread, and pizza. The best way you can avoid this is to switch it with sprouted whole grain bread, brown rice, and quinoa pasta. You can also consider homemade alternative pizza crusts made from sweet potatoes, quinoa, rice, or cauliflower.

Commandment #2 Avoid white sugar

Being on a plant-based diet does not only mean that you consume plant-based foods. It also means healthy living. It is important that you do your best to avoid the habit of needing to sweeten every drink you consume. Whenever you feel the need to do it, choose maple syrup, dates, agave nectar syrup, and fruits - all of which offer natural and somewhat healthier approaches to sweetening.

Note that white sugars and artificial sweeteners of any form have been shown to contribute to weight gain, tooth cavities, excess caloric intake, and even heart disease.

Commandment #3 Keep fake meat products to a minimum

When you first started a plant-based or vegan diet, you may have relied heavily on fake meat products because they tasted great, were quick fixes, and offered a lot of help when transitioning to a plant-based diet. With time, you have managed to reduce them to a bare minimum, perhaps by increasing your ability to cook balanced, natural foods that cover all your protein and nutrient needs. One thing you need to realize is that foods like veggie burgers, veggie meatballs, strips, and fake chicken patties, among others, are heavily processed, with unnecessary ingredients, preservatives, and fillers.

Try as much as you can to avoid them. That is what plant-based truly means!

Commandment #4 Keep no junk food in the house

One thing I believe in is getting rid of temptation. Getting started on a plant-based diet in itself is challenging, and that is why you need to keep all sources of temptation away from you as much as you can. When you are shopping at the store, resist the urge to buy junk food and snacks because if you do, you will definitely end up eating them.

It doesn't matter what you try to tell yourself - this is a feat! It will happen. If you truly need to reward yourself with a treat - something that is perfectly acceptable from time to time - you simply get off the couch, head to the store, and get it. When you get rid of the temptation - from the pantry and fridge - you will be amazed at how it doesn't even cross your mind in the first place.

Commandment #5 Never cook with low-quality cooking oils

I love cooking with healthy plant-based oils like coconut oil, avocado oils, palm oils, and even extra virgin olive oil. When you go for unnatural refined cooking oils, you risk altering your body cell's fatty acid composition, which can contribute to inflammations. This, in turn, increases your risk of developing serious diseases.

Chapter 5: Benefits of a plant-based diet

"The Gods created certain kinds of beings to replenish our bodies; they are the trees and the plants and the seeds."— Plato

Consuming a plant-based diet goes a long way in helping people lose weight. That said, the plant-based diet also offers a wide array of additional health benefits. For starters, consuming a plant-based diet plays a significant role in helping you have a healthy heart, protection against type 2 diabetes, and certain types of cancers. Here are some of the benefits you stand to gain when you switch to plant-based.

A plant-based diet is rich in certain nutrients

Switching to a plant-based diet from a typical Western diet plays a significant role in eliminating meat and animal products. This will mean you rely heavily on other foods. Replacement, in this case, takes the form of fruits, whole grains, beans, nuts, veggies, peas, and seeds, among others.

Considering that these foods make up a large proportion of the plant-based diet compared to the Western diet, this contributes a great deal to a high daily intake of beneficial nutrients. According to several studies, a plant-based diet offers more fiber, antioxidants, and other nutrients that are present in plant foods. They are also said to be loaded with such minerals as folate, potassium, Vitamins A, C, and E, and magnesium, among others.

That said, not all plant-based diets are created the same way. For example, if your plant-based diet is poorly planned, this may contribute to you consuming insufficient amounts of Vitamin B12, fatty acids, zinc, iron, and iodine.

This is why you should try as much as you can to stay away from nutrient-poor, fast-food vegan options. It is important that you base your diet on nutrient-rich whole foods derived from plants and foods that are fortified. It is also advisable that you take Vitamin B12 supplements to ensure that your daily dietary requirements are met.

The bottom line here is that whole food plant-based diets are rich in nutrients, and it is important that you ensure you are eating the right foods and have a well-planned diet to get all the nutrients your body needs.

A plant-based diet helps you lose excess weight

Today, many people are turning to a plant-based diet with the hope of shedding those stubborn extra pounds. This is often for a good reason too. According to several observational studies, vegans tend to be thinner and have a lower body mass index (BMI) than people who are nonvegans.

Several randomized controlled studies, which are the gold standard in scientific research, show that consuming a vegan diet is more effective in stimulating weight loss when compared to other diets. In one study, a vegan managed to lose 4.2 kg more than someone on a control diet over 18 weeks. What was even more interesting was that participants who were on a vegan diet managed to lose more weight compared to those who were on a calorie-restricted diet - even when vegans were allowed to eat their fill.

According to a recent study that compared the weight loss effects of five different diets, there was evidence that vegan and vegetarian diets were accepted as much as semi-vegetarian and Western diets were. Even when people were not adhering to their diets, the semi-vegetarian and vegans still managed to lose slightly more weight than those on a standard Western diet.

The bottom line is that vegan diets naturally lower your calorie intake without you actively having to focus on cutting calories as you would with other diets.

A plant-based diet lowers blood sugar levels and improves kidney function

When you go totally plant-based, one of the benefits for someone with type 2 diabetes and deteriorating kidney function is that their blood sugar levels improve alongside their kidney function.

According to research, it is evident that vegans have lower blood sugar levels, high insulin-sensitivity, and a lower risk of developing type 2 diabetes by between 50-78%. Several studies demonstrate that vegan diets lower blood sugar levels in people with diabetes according to reports by ADA, AHA, and NCEP. In one study, at least 43% of research participants following a vegan diet had a reduction in the dosage of blood sugar lowering medication vs. 26% in a group that followed ADA-recommended diets.

Another study showed that diabetics who substituted meat for plant proteins had a lower risk of developing kidney complications. Several studies demonstrate that consuming a plant-based diet goes a long way in offering relief of systemic distal polyneuropathy symptoms, a condition characterized by burning and sharp pain among diabetics.

The bottom line here is that plant-based diets lower the risk of developing type 2 diabetes. Additionally, they are effective in lowering blood sugar levels and help a great deal in preventing further medical complications.

A plant-based diet may protect against certain cancers

According to reports by the WHO, approximately a third of cancers can be prevented by factors that are within our control, and diet is one of them. For instance, when you consume legumes regularly, you stand to lower the risk of developing colorectal cancer by 9-18%. Research also shows that consuming at least seven portions of fresh veggies and fruits daily lowers the risk of cancer deaths by up to 15%.

The good thing about a plant-based diet is that you get to consume a considerable amount more of fruits, legumes, and veggies compared to non-vegans. This explains why, in a recent review of 96 studies, it was shown that vegans benefit a great deal from consuming a plant-based diet by lowering their risk of cancer death by 15%. The thing is that plant-based diets contain soy products that offer protection against breast cancer.

When you avoid certain animal products, you also lower the risk of developing cancers such as colon, prostate, or breast cancer. This may be because a vegan diet is free of smoked or processed meats and meats that have been prepared by subjecting them to higher temperatures - thought to stimulate cancer cells. Vegans also benefit from consuming foods free from dairy that have been shown to increase the risk of developing prostate cancer.

A plant-based diet lowers the risk of heart disease

Consuming fresh veggies, fruits, legumes, and fiber is associated with a lower risk of developing heart disease. When your plant-based diet is well-planned, you set yourself up to consume more of these foods.

According to observational studies that compare vegans and vegetarians in the general population, there is evidence that points to vegans having a 75% lower risk of developing high blood pressure. Additionally, vegans have been shown to have a 42% lower risk of dying from heart disease. Several randomized controlled studies have also demonstrated that vegan diets are effective in lowering blood sugar levels, total cholesterol, and LDL cholesterol compared to other types of diets.

When blood pressure, cholesterol, and blood sugar levels are reduced, the risk of heart disease is also reduced by about 46%. As opposed to the general population, vegans consume high quantities of whole grains and nuts, which have been shown to be good for the heart.

A plant-based diet reduces arthritis pain

According to a few studies, there is evidence that consuming a plant-based diet has a positive effect on arthritis. One study of 40 arthritic participants, in which some continued their omnivorous diet, and others switched to a whole food, plant-based diet over six weeks, showed that vegans reported higher energy levels and improved body functioning compared to those who did not change their diet.

According to two studies that investigated the effect of probiotic-rich, raw-food plant-based diets on people with rheumatoid arthritis, there was evidence that showed participants in the plant-based diet group had improved symptoms – like reductions in joint swelling, pain, and morning stiffness - as opposed to those who did not change their diet.

The bottom line here is that a plant-based diet formed on probiotic-rich whole foods significantly lowers the symptoms of rheumatoid arthritis and osteoarthritis.

Improved metabolism

As we have already mentioned, a plant-based diet benefits from increased consumption of fresh veggies and fruits, which have essential nutrients. The good thing about a plant-based diet is that it is high in fiber, folic acid, Vitamins E and C, magnesium, and phytochemicals. Additionally, plant-based foods are low in saturated fats, cholesterol, and calories.

According to studies, a plant-based diet improves energy and metabolism in obese, healthy, and type 2 diabetic individuals. Consuming a plant-based diet stimulates favorable changes in the gut microbiome. There is also evidence that shows that consuming a plant-based diet offers protective nutrients and phytochemicals.

How to stay healthy while eating a plant-based diet

Studies show that even 15 minutes of activity a couple of times each week is advantageous. Yet, in a perfect world, you ought to get 30 minutes of exercise four or five times each week. The most significant thing is beginning, however, so put on your gym shoes—it's an ideal opportunity to get going!

Obviously, attempting to accomplish a wellness objective on practice alone is only part of the battle. Eating an integral plant-based diet means you achieve results more rapidly.

In this part, I address how being active is an advantage for well-being. I likewise detail how exercise supplements your plant-based diet. Eating a deeply nutritious plant-based diet alongside doing a regular exercise routine is the formula for astonishing well-being! The advantages are various, so we should get into them.

The benefits of regular exercise

Being active helps your cardiovascular well-being, absorption, and skin, and it likewise gives you upbeat endorphins to fuel your day with energy, liveliness, and force. Exercise can be addictive in the best way!

You needn't bother with a costly gym enrollment and high-market equipment to get fit as a fiddle. Your exercises can be as short as twenty minutes per day. Regardless of whether you're a top competitor or a fitness newbie, you can generally find space for assortment and balance. Simply remember: Working out shouldn't feel like an errand; it should be fun.

Any activity is superior to no activity, and a lot of the time, you need to begin simply. If you aren't particularly fit or don't exercise much, start with just a 10-minute stroll a couple of times each week. As you become increasingly used to the movement, go for longer strolls or walk more quickly.

Improves well-being

The impact that activity has on an individual's well-being is difficult to describe in words. It's that euphoric feeling you get after you've finished an exercise. Exercise can help:

- Relieve stress and tension.

- Slow age-related decay. Exercise builds your stamina, bone and muscle quality, and balance, which all become increasingly reduced as you age.

- Promote inward harmony. Exercise stimulates you intellectually and helps you learn to love yourself.

Something else to consider is that you should set aside a period to relax during the day, especially if the day has been monotonous. Do yoga or meditation in the morning or night. Yoga can assist you in making a psychological and physical connection within your body.

Your plant-based diet can likewise improve well-being, which is why many people associate plant diets with reflection. Additionally, because plants are anything but difficult to process, a plant-based diet makes it simpler to contemplate and loosen up your psyche and body.

Creates and boosts energy

Did you realize that working out gives you more energy? New research suggests that regular exercise can build energy levels, even among individuals with weakness-related ailments, for example, malignancy and coronary illness.

Specialists state that people with a wide variety of conditions can all benefit from regular exercise.

To help your physical movement, plant-based foods give you all the full-scale supplements (proteins, sugars, and fats) that are basic in boosting and keeping up the energy you gain from working out. Since working out leads to physical pressure, it produces acidity in the body. Your plant-based diet enables your body to counteract that and revert to a condition of alkalinity.

The following are a selection of my favorite plant-based energy-boosting foods. These are the foods I grab when I need to get going, and I very much recommend them to any individual who hasn't tried them yet. I know that my body's going to use them to give me that increase in energy without me crashing. They support me, nourish me, and are easy enough to prepare that I can eat them every day in different ways and never get bored.

Check this out!

Food Choice	Health Benefits
Hemp seeds	Contain omega-3 fats and provide energy that lasts. Prepare them with mixed greens, in smoothies, and with grains.
Chia seeds	Are packed with fiber and expand when

drenched. Chia makes the tastiest morning porridge. Astounding as a pre-exercise food.

Kale	This is a green verdant powerhouse veggie. It's packed with magnesium. Cut up with mixed greens or steam as an afterthought with quinoa - kale finishes any plate.
Sea vegetables	Containing a broad scope of minerals and supplements, ocean vegetables provide sodium. My preferred ocean vegetables are arame and nori – they provide mental clarity.
Tempeh	This is perhaps the most noteworthy source of plant protein, is matured, and is anything but difficult to process. I love marinating tempeh with vinegar, lemon juice, and coconut oil for a lift to dishes of mixed greens and wraps.
Coconut water and coconut oil	Coconut water renews the body with much-needed electrolytes. So when you're working out, this ought to be your go-to drink. Coconut oil is packed with medium-chain fats, so it's a snappy source of energy and sustenance when on the move.
Quinoa	Contains all the fundamental amino acids, which allow for protein absorption. Protein assembles muscle, so it's critical to consume, particularly after exercise.
Goji berries	Are a source of cancer-prevention agents, protein, and fiber. They're flawless before exercise or extraordinary in a smoothie after

	exercise.
Cacao	One of nature's most extravagant sources of magnesium. It gives a characteristic increase in energy, and it's a good excuse to have some chocolate. In a smoothie or grain, it gives the ideal crunch and a kick.

Improves digestion

Being active helps support digestion by making your muscles work harder, which burns more calories and helps keep your weight in check. Try to combine the following two types of exercise:

Cardio includes short explosions of high-power activity (for instance, running, cycling, etc.) for a while, followed by a rest period. You repeat this for somewhere in the range of 15 to 30 minutes for a digestion-boosting exercise.

Weight work is about your body pushing or pulling weight (for example, lifting weights). This gets your muscles working rapidly to help support digestion. Truth be told, your muscles continue to consume energy (calories) long after you've quit working out!

Here again, your plant-based diet is the ideal partner for your exercises. To truly boost your digestion, eat foods grown from the ground. These contain fiber, water, vitamins and minerals and can reinforce your cells.

Whole grains are also acceptable, as they have a moderate amount of glucose, some protein, B vitamins, minerals, and fiber. Vegetables and beans contain proteins that are integral to grain proteins, B vitamins, minerals, fiber, and cancer prevention agents. Nuts and seeds have basic unsaturated fats, great quality protein, vitamins, minerals, and fiber. These will be major contributors to boosting your digestion.

Enjoy these top digestion-boosting plant-based foods:

Food Choice	Health Benefit
Grapefruit	Grapefruit helps "fire up" your digestion by advancing insulin obstruction and weight reduction. Have some grapefruit before a meal, and see how it benefits you.
Green tea	It's not the caffeine in green tea that assists digestion but instead the cancer prevention agent family called catechins. They have a thermogenic impact that advances fat consumption. Consider drinking some green tea in the first part of the day a couple of times each week (or more).
Ginger	Ginger is an energizer, so it helps support digestion and increases energy - particularly during exercise. Ginger likewise stifles cortisol (a steroid hormone that is required to manage energy) generation, eases pressure, and helps prevent weight gain.

Avocado	Maybe you're thinking, "How does this consume fat if it is a fat?" Well, the fats in avocados are polyunsaturated and monounsaturated fats, which increase your basal metabolic rate - accelerating your digestion in any event. The fat in avocados is likewise very satisfying and may help control cravings for less healthy foods.

Boosts immunity

Regular physical activity can help your body ward off diseases, alongside other medical issues, for example, coronary illness, osteoporosis, and malignancy. Here are a couple of speculations concerning why this is:

-   Physical movement may help flush microscopic organisms from the lungs (preventing colds and influenza) and by allowing the body to process more waste, for example, through urine and sweat.

- Exercise enables antibodies (white platelets) to move around the body more quickly. Along these lines, they can recognize diseases faster than usual. Our body is brilliant, and these cells, in some way or another, have a method for "noticing" different cells from interfering microorganisms or infections.

- The increase in internal heat level during activity may slow down bacterial development, allowing the body to battle contamination more adequately (like when you have a fever).

- Exercise hinders stress-related hormones. Stress frequently leads to sickness.

Even though activity is beneficial, don't overdo it. This might be counterproductive because it diminishes the level of white platelets in the body and can stimulate stress-related hormones.

Forestalls ailment

Exercise deeply affects the counteraction and treatment of interminable maladies, for example, coronary illness, malignant growth, and diabetes. Exercise can help counterbalance sicknesses by advancing lymph development through the body, allowing more waste to be processed, and triggering hormones that positively affect all areas of the body.

Alongside regular exercise, living on a plant-based diet diminishes your risk of oxidative pressure and incessant aggravation, which are huge causes behind numerous ceaseless sicknesses. Various specialists agree that constant aggravation of the mind from unreasonable oxidative pressure is a significant reason behind specific mental issues, from simple lack of concentration to Alzheimer's disease. Too much oxidative pressure can be activated by gluten prejudice or affectability brought about by an unbalanced gut. Different causes incorporate casein (a dairy-based protein), food hypersensitivities and sensitivities, lacking cancer prevention agents, and unnecessary animal-based protein consumption.

Don't think, just move

The way to begin is to simply begin. Discover something to do and get your body going. The more time you spend considering what physical activity you want to do, the more you're delaying making your body better. It's alright if you don't know whether you like something; just try it! The best way to see whether you like it is to give it a go. If you realize you don't like it, just switch to another activity. Keep doing this until you find what suits you.

If you're really unsure of what physical activity to do, how long to do it for, or if you're worried about any underlying conditions being affected by exercise – seek out an expert. This could be a personal trainer, for example, or even a doctor. Make sure you don't do anything that could worsen a condition you already have.

The objective is to have a great time, feel better, and get results!

Many individuals enjoy simple strolling or running since it's such a simple method to work out. Cheap too!

Remember, though, that repetitive high-impact movement can cause you issues. Educating yourself can help you avoid any damage, especially to your joints. The best thing to do is practice a variety of activities, and try to exercise as many different muscle groups as you can. Switch up throughout the week, and you should be golden.

Three fantastic oxygen-consuming exercises are cycling, swimming, and hiking. These exercises are all relatively low-impact, so if you have issues in your joints or you're overweight, these will be far easier for you. You can also use these to move onto more intense exercises in the future if you're a beginner – hiking or walking can become running, for example. Or cycling down a country pathway can turn into cycling through steep hills. Swimming is generally very soft on your body, despite working out all of your muscles.

Weight-based and body-weight exercises

These exercises are helpful for such a large number of reasons. Notwithstanding building muscle, they can help you burn more calories, strengthen bone quality and well-being, and get the blood pumping too.

Here are some of the most popular activities you can start with:

- Medicine ball

- Sit-ups

- Body-weight squats and thrusts

- Resistance band work

- Floor work (yoga, Pilates, stretching)

- Kettle ball

- Planks

- Push-ups

- Weight machines at the gym

- Free weights

Floor work is a broad term for full-body exercises and stretching techniques that work your body from head to toe. Some forms of floor work incorporate yoga, Pilates, and general stretching. Floor work has numerous phenomenal advantages, including toning and increasing flexibility, which will benefit many people.

Perhaps the most significant advantage is in the cool-down part — it will leave you feeling inspired and fulfilled after your work-out! During this time, you can also stretch and breathe out all of your stresses and anxieties, helping you to feel a greater connection with your body.

When you develop a mind-body connection, your body builds mindfulness, which is especially advantageous if you play sports, need to have a superior understanding of your body, or find yourself sore a lot and have no idea why.

You can also choose to join a class if you want to do your exercise with other people, or do it alone and stay peaceful and quiet.

Group activities

Doing things solo may not be your thing, so join a group! You might be one of those individuals who grew up playing hockey, baseball, or football, and so aren't used to being alone. As a part of your daily routine, taking part in group activities has a wide range of advantages (not merely the high physical movement level, which is an immense advantage, obviously). Group activities allow you to mingle, learn teamwork, and develop yourself alongside others.

Another benefit is that you have others keeping you responsible and anticipating that you should be there, so you're less likely to skip out. It also gives you something to look forward to every week.

Here are probably the most well-known group activities to try out:

- Football
- Tennis
- Basketball
- Baseball or softball
- Volleyball
- Hockey
- Soccer

Living your best plant-based life

If you're newly enrolled in college, you already have a lot going on - navigating a new place, meeting new people, following a new schedule, and more. And, at the same time, you might be learning to cook for yourself and figuring out how to stock your kitchen - if you are lucky enough to have one!

It's easy to let your diet slip when living on your own for the first time - because, let's be honest, junk food is often cheaper, faster, and more of a temptation. It's a major problem in our society that a fast-food burger costs less than a salad. Plus, with no parents around to monitor your eating, it's easy to fall into whatever eating habits your friends have (like late-night pizza).

In several studies, vegans have been shown to have lower total cholesterol, LDL cholesterol, triglycerides, and blood pressure than meat-eaters and vegetarians - all risk factors for cardiovascular disease, which is the leading cause of death in the United States.

The thing is, you will feel so much better, have more energy, and set yourself up for a healthier life if you make conscious choices about what you put into your body. Once you master the basics of the plant-based diet, you'll see it's not as difficult as you might have imagined, and the effort to learn is worth it. There is absolutely nothing I regret, or feel deprived of, as a vegan. I only wish I'd started sooner! If you want to start or continue a plant-based lifestyle while getting your education, here are five ideas to keep you motivated.

Health

One of the most important choices you can make for your health is to eat more plants. Vegetarians generally have a lower risk of cardiovascular disease, obesity, type 2 diabetes, and some cancers. Bonus: Eliminating dairy can potentially clear up chronic acne.

Budget

There are certainly ways to spend a lot of money on vegan comfort foods, like coconut ice cream and frozen pizzas, but remember that the areas of the world with the least money and resources frequently eat plant-based diets. If you focus on basic whole foods like beans, rice, and most of the other ingredients in this book, you'll probably spend less than your omnivore friends.

Environment

Going plant-based is the single biggest thing you can do to reduce your environmental footprint. A person following a vegan diet produces the equivalent of 50 percent less carbon dioxide, uses 1/11 the oil, 1/13 the water, and 1/18 the land for their food compared to a meat-eater. The impact of animal agriculture is so broad: It is the leading cause of land degradation, air pollution, water shortage, biodiversity loss, species extinction, water pollution, and habitat destruction.

Social Justice

We're already growing enough food to feed more than the world's population, but much of the grains and soy we grow are fed to animals for meat and dairy production. In countries where children are starving, food is being fed to the animals they raise to sell as meat to other countries. Animal agriculture has taken over or destroyed the habitat of wild animals and fish, which indigenous populations rely on for survival. Privileged societies have access to a seemingly endless supply of food in grocery stores, but we don't often see the real cost of those foods we put in our carts.

<u>Animals</u>

I've put this last because it's probably the most obvious, but it is the most common reason why people go fully vegan. Animals are raised in horrifying conditions and are either killed to be eaten, killed as a by-product of agriculture (like male chicks who are killed at egg factories), or exploited in unnatural ways their whole lives (like being given hormones or having their babies taken away so they will produce more milk and eggs).

Since we don't need meat, fish, poultry, eggs, or dairy to get the nutrients we need, why not make choices that help avoid this unnecessary cruelty?

Chapter 6: Essential Tips for Beginners

"By eating meat, we share the responsibility of climate change, the destruction of our forests, and the poisoning of our air and water. The simple act of becoming a vegetarian will make a difference in the health of our planet."— Thích Nhất

When you're starting out on a plant-based diet, there can be several challenges along the way. There is a lot of confusing information online on what is the right way to transition to a plant-based diet. Trust me, the amount of information out there is overwhelming, and you might get lost in the middle of it all.

When I decided to start with a plant-based diet a couple of years ago, I had no idea where to start. Just like you, I was confused about what the right or wrong way was when approaching this transition. What am I supposed to eat? What does "enough" calories even mean? How will my body adjust to these changes? What kind of foods should I focus on eating, and which ones should I avoid?

Well, after several trials and errors, I finally figured the main things that a person on a plant-based diet or vegan should consume.

Here, I will give you some of the tips that worked for me and have worked for several people I have shared them with too.

Come with me.

Prepare yourself

When you decide to go totally plant-based, it is important that you conduct a little bit of research beforehand. This is a critical step in ensuring that you know where to start so that you can develop the right mindset for a plant-based diet. This will also help you understand the kinds of foods you are supposed to focus on when you start. After all, the plant-based food pyramid is completely different from the conventional one you were taught in school.

It is also important that you conduct a little research on local stores and restaurants that offer plant-based food. Check out the food variations they offer and other specialized vegan foods options they might have. Whenever you feel confused about what to buy to fill up your pantry, our grocery list (in the next chapter) will help guide you in the right direction.

Realize that learning is a continuous process. Once you are on the plant-based path, it is important that you keep expanding your knowledge. It could be discovering new cooking methods or other vegan food options available in the market. Whatever it is, ensure that you are constantly learning something new that will make your life easier every day.

Starting a plant-based diet is a new and exciting adventure you have embarked on, and there are lots of things to discover, ensure that you don't miss out on anything!

Start at a pace that best suits you

One of the biggest mistakes people make is jumping right into a plant-based diet without really thinking about it critically - what they really wish to achieve. It is important that you consider all factors and why you are interested in a plant-based diet so that you can establish a solid foundation for the time to come. When you have all these factors considered, you can get started on a plant-based diet and never look back!

That said, some people need to go through a gradual transition to make things easier for them. The first step is to eliminate red meat from your diet during the first week. Then move on to white meat - fish and poultry - and so on. You can also do this as a challenge – if you decide to start with a plant-based diet or even vegan and never look back, a challenge is the best way to avoid getting overwhelmed. When you achieve your challenge successfully, you will be more confident embarking on a plant-based diet for life.

That said, you don't have to throw yourself into a challenge. You can start at a pace that works best for you and then take baby steps. You can start with the one-week challenge, then progress to two weeks, a month, three months, six months, a year, and so on, until it is ingrained in you.

Keep your meals simple and diverse

When you embark on a plant-based diet, it is easy to want to overcomplicate things here and there. Most people jump straight into the world of wanting to make every meal fancy and expensive - vegan cheese, vegan meat, and milk alternatives. You may be tempted to want to try complicated vegan recipes, and then when you fail, you beat yourself.

While there is so much fun in being creative, the easiest way to go about it is to keep everything simple. Ask yourself whether you really want to do it. Realize that you don't have to focus on preparing complicated and time-consuming vegan foods when starting out. Embrace beauty in simplicity.

It is important that you focus your attention on consuming whole foods - grains, legumes, vegetables, fruits, starches, seeds, and nuts, among others. It is also important that you try consuming different kinds of foods that will offer your body a full range of minerals, vitamins, and antioxidants.

Think about your workplace and how it supports your new diet. Are there places where you can get a vegan meal for lunch at the workplace? If not, then the best thing is for you to whip up something the evening before that you can bring with you to the workplace. Trust me; you will save some money and still fill your stomach with something healthy and satisfying.

Learn about plant-based food alternatives

When you are transitioning to a plant-based diet, you might be tempted to think that you will never be able to enjoy the eggs and cheese you love. This is especially the case when you have grown up with all these flavors. There will be times when you will crave these things. There are times when you will feel confused about baking your favorite desserts without necessarily adding in eggs or dairy products.

Well, if that happens, realize that there are several excellent plant-based/vegan food alternatives you can choose from to replace these ingredients or give you all the flavors you want in your vegan food. The truth is that as a vegan, you can create your own cheese that tastes just like your favorite cheese. Trust me; you don't have to miss the old tastes again!

Embrace the changes in your body. We are all unique individuals. Just because you are on a plant-based diet doesn't mean that you will feel the same as someone else on it. You are not going to experience the same changes as the other person. The truth is that each of our bodies responds to a plant-based diet in different ways. According to research, the very first few days after switching to a plant-based diet, the body gets into a detox mode.

There is a chance that you will experience headaches and shifts in energy levels. This is perfectly normal, and you don't need to panic. Understand that the body has excellent ways of adapting to these changes, and all you have to do is give it some time. If you have been a heavy meat- eater for most of your childhood, teenagerhood or adulthood, the chances are that your body will definitely go through a period of detox.

You don't have to worry about this too much. The symptoms you are experiencing at this time are eventually going to disappear after a month or so. As soon as your body adjusts to the new lifestyle, you will be back to normal - as if nothing ever happened. That said, if there is something you feel uncomfortable with, the best thing is for you to seek the help of a specialist.

Load up on healthy snacks

Remember that plant-based foods tend to be lower in calories compared to animal products. This means that when you are on a plant-based diet, you must ensure that you are fueling your body. It is important that you don't starve yourself. Yes, this will take some getting used to - a new diet, new meal size, and frequencies - but it will all fall into place eventually.

The best thing is for you to ensure that you load up on healthy snacks such as fruits and nuts. Healthy snacks will help your body adjust naturally and keep your cravings down as much as possible. So, when you are leaving for work in the morning, ensure that you bring some with you so that you can consume them on the go.

Learn to read the food labels

At the beginning of your plant-based journey, you will read lots of food labels. There are companies that do a great job adding in a little title on what is suitable for vegans – which is suitable for people on a plant-based diet. Others put special vegan logos on their packages so that you can easily know whether the product is right for you or not.

However, several food products out there do not have food labels or any specific markings that allow you to read the ingredients. The truth is that most of these foods are likely to have animal products in them, such as potato chips, beer, and certain orange juice brands. There are those that are harder to detect than others. If you are a vegan and you do it mainly for the animals, beware of these non-vegan ingredients like albumen, gelatin, lactose, and casein, among others.

The best thing you can do is to download a vegan app. Simply type "is it vegan" in the Apple store or Android Play Store (there is a selection of different apps). And use it to scan the ingredient list.

Show yourself a little compassion

People often strive for perfection. Well, if this is you, then you better stop. It is important to remember that you are human just like the rest of us, and because of that, you will make mistakes here and there. You may buy a food that has animal ingredients in it without knowing. You may eat out at a restaurant that serves bread with butter on top of it without knowing.

When one of my friends first started out on a vegan diet, she used to drink soy milk before she discovered that that particular brand had actual cow milk on its ingredient list. What am I saying? When you get started on a vegan diet, you might be blinded by the fact that something has been labeled 100% soy milk when, in fact, there is an animal-derived ingredient in it. Realize that this is not your mistake, and all you can do is give yourself a break and find another product that suits your vegan lifestyle.

The trick is for you to accept all the mistakes that happen and find a way to move past them. Just because you made a small mistake does not mean that you should give up. What you must note is that going on a vegan diet is not a pledge of perfection, and this is the very reason why you should practice showing yourself a little compassion. You will start to see how helpful it is to read labels thoroughly and go through the vegan ingredient list before you commit to buying a product.

Join a community of like-minded people

Do you have friends or family who follow a plant-based diet? Are there people at work you know who are transitioning to a plant-based diet? If you feel isolated, it is important that you try and create a community with these people. The best thing for each one of you is to share your experiences. Within this community, people get to ask questions, open up about their challenges, and how they managed to overcome them, draw inspiration from others, and seek support where they need it.

My husband doesn't eat plant-based, but most of the time, I feed him plant-based or vegetarian food, and he likes it, or he doesn't even realize that there is no meat. Of course, he requires meat, so I still have to cook it for him sometimes. So, if you have a husband or wife at home who doesn't share your plant-based/vegan views, I understand how hard it is, and especially if they aren't supportive. But we can give them the information, we can "teach" them, but we can't force them, we have to wait patiently and see if one day they will join us. If you have somebody like this at home, the journey is twice as hard, and it requires twice as much effort.

When I started this diet, my husband didn't want to eat anything plant-based except salad, he only wanted meat, and it was hard, as I had to cook two different meals every day. I got exhausted and gave up and started eating meat again, and for a long time, it was like this - on and off.

With time I gained more knowledge, I got smart, I learned that I could use the same recipe, only remove meat, etc. I cooked the same food, I fed him the meat option and I ate the non-meat option. Now he even eats plant-based food as my recipes got better! So, there is hope!

Realize that the community can be beneficial both offline and online. Personally, I follow lots of vegans across the world on social media platforms like Facebook and Instagram. I like drawing inspiration from their delicious plant-based/vegan recipes, meal plans, and shopping tips. This is what keeps me motivated to keep going. I get to ask questions where I feel challenged and get people's experiences.

The truth is, there is nothing you will go through as a vegan at the beginning that is unique to you. There are people out there who have gone through what you are currently experiencing. If you join a community and share your challenges, thoughts, and dilemmas, you can find someone out there who can inspire you to be better. Today, choose to connect with vegan lovers out there and grow your knowledge in this area. Remember that once you are ready to hop onto a vegan path, there are several other things you can do to make the way easier.

Equip yourself with knowledge through comprehensive research before you jump right into a plant-based diet. Then pick a pace that is right for you. If you like to go with the all-or-nothing concept, then the chances are that you will be able to become a vegan overnight. However, if you are like me and like to take baby steps, embrace gradual transitions by slowly eliminating more and more animal products from your diet every day.

The last thing you want is to complicate things for yourself. When you are just starting out with a plant-based diet, keep everything about your meals diverse and straightforward. The best place to start is to learn the essential plant-based alternative options so that you can seamlessly replace all animal-derived ingredients and products with plant-based alternatives you like.

Remember that you have taken a journey of compassion with yourself. This means that whenever you make a mistake, you have to accept it to move on. Don't beat yourself up because you have been consuming a food you thought was vegan only to find that it has animal ingredients in them. Cut yourself a little slack and remember that you are only human.

Finally, find a plant-based community that can support you on this journey. When you surround yourself with like-minded people, you will not only feel protected but also motivated to be yourself and have some fun too.

Chapter 7: Simple Vegan Recipes

Breakfast Recipes

Apple Oatmeal

Prep time: 5 minutes ~ Cooking time: 20 minutes ~ Servings: 2

Ingredients

1 cup cut oats
2 teaspoon coconut oil
1 cup apples, chopped
2 ½ cup water
3 tablespoon brown sugar
1 teaspoon vanilla extract
½ teaspoon ground cinnamon

Directions

1. Press the Sauté mode on your instant pot.
2. Place the coconut oil, apples, brown sugar, vanilla extract, and ground cinnamon in the instant pot. (If you don't have an instant pot, you can cook it as normal)
3. Add cut oats and stir.
4. Sauté the mixture for 4-5 minutes. Stir it from time to time.
5. Then add water and mix it up.
6. Close the lid and press Manual mode (High pressure).
7. Cook the oatmeal for 13 minutes on High.
8. Then make quick pressure release.
9. Mix up the meal well before serving.

You can decorate your oatmeal with fruit, nuts, seeds of your choice.

Nutrition value/serving: calories 236, fat 6.2, fiber 5, carbs 42.9, protein 6.2

Savory Chickpea Omelet

Prep Time: 10 Minutes ~ Cook Time: 25-30 Minutes ~ Servings: 12

Ingredients

Olive oil, for preparing the muffin tin
2 cups chickpea flour
1 teaspoon salt
1 teaspoon baking powder (optional —makes them fluffier)
2 ½ cups water
1 tablespoon nutritional yeast (optional)
1 teaspoon dried herbs (optional)
½ teaspoon smoked paprika (optional) teaspoon garlic powder (optional)
½ teaspoon onion powder (optional)
2 cups chopped vegetables, such as zucchini, carrot,
bell pepper, mushrooms, onion, com, peas, and olives
1 cup chopped spinach or kale (stems removed)

Directions

1. Preheat the oven to 400°F. Coat a muffin tin with olive oil, line with paper muffin cups, or use a nonstick tin.
2. In a large bowl, combine the chickpea flour, salt, and baking powder (if using). Add the water and stir thoroughly to combine. You don't want any chunks of chickpea flour. The

batter will be fairly runny. If using any optional seasonings, add them here and stir to combine.

3. Stir the veggies and spinach into the batter. Scoop the batter into the prepared tin, about 1/3 cup for each muffin. Bake for 25 to 30 minutes, until lightly browned on top. If you prefer them slightly gooey on the inside, take them out of the oven after 25 minutes; if you like them firmer, keep them in for 30 minutes.

4. Let cool for 10 minutes. Run a dinner knife around the inside of each cup to loosen, then tilt the cups on their sides in the muffin wells, so air gets underneath. These keep in an airtight container in the refrigerator for about five days or in the freezer indefinitely—thaw before reheating.

Nutritional facts: Calories: 66; Protein: 4g; Total fat: 1g; Saturated fat: 0g; Carbohydrates: 10g; Fiber: 2g

Zucchini-Potato Hash Browns

Prep Time: 10 Minutes ~ Cooking Time: 25-30 Minutes ~ Servings: 4

Ingredients

1 potato, scrubbed or peeled and grated
½ zucchini, grated
2 tablespoons all-purpose flour
Salt to taste, divided
Freshly ground black pepper
1 scallion, chopped, or 1 teaspoon onion powder (optional)
1 to 2 teaspoons olive oil
Salt

Directions

1. In a large bowl, combine the grated potato and zucchini. Sprinkle with salt and toss to combine. Push the vegetables to one side of the bowl and squeeze them to drain off some of the moisture, tipping the bowl to drain into the sink.
2. Add the flour, a pinch each of salt and pepper, and the scallion (if using), and toss to mix.
3. Place a large skillet over medium-high heat. While it heats, form the zucchini-potato mixture into 4 balls in the bowl.
4. Add the olive oil to the skillet and flatten the balls into the oiled pan. Cook for 5 to 7 minutes, until lightly browned on one side.
5. Flip and cook the other side until lightly browned.

Nutritional facts: Calories: 78; Protein: 2g; Total fat: 2g; Saturated fat: 0g; Carbohydrates: 14g; Fiber: 2g

Main Dishes

Vegan Hamburger

Great news! You can still eat a burger even as a vegan! Simply swap the beefburger for a plant-based option and cheese for a vegan cheese. You have two options - you can go to your local store and pick up a vegan burger from a freezer, or you can make your own. In case you decide to make your own, here is a recipe from tasty.co, which is one of my favorite websites when it comes to food (Tasty Vegan).

Prep time: 30 minutes ~ Cooking time: 20 minutes ~ Servings: 4

Ingredients

1 cup walnuts (100 g)
8 oz cremini mushroom (225 g)
2 tablespoons olive oil, divided
2 tablespoons low sodium soy sauce
½ teaspoon cumin
1 yellow onion, diced
2 cloves garlic, minced
1 teaspoon salt
½ teaspoon red bell pepper
1 tablespoon tomato paste
1 cup black beans (170 g), cooked
3 tablespoons beet, grated
1 cup brown rice (230 g), cooked
1 tablespoon vegan mayonnaise
1 teaspoon vegan Worcestershire
1 teaspoon liquid smoke

½ cup vital wheat gluten (6 5 g)
Vegan BBQ sauce, for basting
4 slices vegan cheese
4 burger buns
Vegan mayonnaise, to serve
Lettuce, to serve
Sliced tomato, to serve
Red onion, sliced, to serve

Directions

1. Add walnuts to the bowl of a food processor and pulse until crumbly. Add mushrooms and blend until finely chopped.
2. In a large skillet over medium heat, add 1 tablespoon olive oil and add the mushroom walnut mixture, cooking for 5-8 minutes or until all moisture has evaporated.
3. Add soy sauce and cumin and cook, occasionally stirring, until dry. Transfer mixture to a bowl. 4. Add 1 tablespoon of olive oil to skillet.
5. Add the onion and cook, occasionally stirring, until semi-translucent, about 3 minutes.
6. Add garlic, salt, pepper, and tomato paste and cook for another 3-5 minutes until fragrant. Set aside.
7. Add black beans and onion mixture to food processor, and blend until mostly smooth.
8. Transfer mixture to bowl and add beets, rice, vegan mayo, Worcestershire sauce, and liquid smoke and stir until combined.
9. Add in vital wheat gluten and use hands to knead burger mixture together until all wheat gluten is fully incorporated.
10. Form burgers into 4 patties about 3-inches (7 cm) in diameter and 1-inch (2 cm) thick.
11. In a large cast-iron pan, over medium-high heat cooks patties about 5 minutes on each side.

12. Add on vegan cheese slices and melt. Assemble burger with vegan mayo, lettuce, tomato, and red onion.

Lentil Lasagna

Prep Time: 15 Minutes ~ Cook Time: 50 Minutes ~ Servings: 1

Ingredients

1 tbsp of olive oil
1 onion (chopped)
1 celery (chopped, stick)
1 carrot (chopped)
1 clove of garlic (crushed)
1 tbsp of com flour
2 cans of 400g lentils (drained, rinsed)
400g of tomato (chopped)
1 tsp of ketchup (mushroom)
1 tsp of vegetable stock (powder)
1 tsp of oregano (chopped)
2 cauliflower (heads, cut into florets and steamed)
2 tbsp of soya milk (unsweetened)
A pinch of grated nutmeg (freshly)
egg-free lasagna sheets (dried)

Directions

1. In a medium saucepan, heat the olive oil and sauté the onion, celery and carrot until softened, 5 minutes. Add the garlic, cook for 2 more minutes, and stir in the com flour and lentils.
2. Pour tomatoes, mushroom ketchup, stock powder, oregano and some seasoning. Bring to a boil for 15 minutes.

3. In a blender, process the cauliflower, soya milk, and nutmeg until smooth.
4. Preheat the oven to 350 F.
5. Layover the base, a ceramic casserole dish, a third of the lentil mixture then fill with a single layer of lasagna sheet. Top with another third of the lentil mixture, then spread over a third of the cauliflower purée, followed by a pasta layer. Finish with the last third of lentils and lasagna, then the remainder of the purée.
6. Cover with foil and bake for 35 to 45 minutes.
7. Remove the dish, foil, and allow cooling for 2 minutes.
8. Serve warm.

Instead of lentils, why don't you try "fake beef"?

Nutritional facts: Calories: 478; Fat: 27.7g; Saturated fat: 7.2g; Carbohydrate: 32g; Fiber: llg; Sugar: 13g; Protein: 29g; Iron: 4mg; Sodium: 604mg

Noodles with Sticky Tofu

Prep Time: 15 Minutes ~ Cook Time: 20 Minutes ~ Servings: 2

Ingredients

1/2 large size cucumber
2 tbsp of pure date sugar
100ml of wine vinegar (rice)
100ml of olive oil
200g pack of tofu (fir, cut into cubes)
2 tbsp of maple syrup
4 tbsp of white miso paste
30g of sesame seeds (white)
250g soba noodles (dried)
2 spring onions, (shredded, garnish)

Directions

1. Cut thin ribbons off the cucumber using a peeler, leaving behind the seeds. In a tub, place the ribbons and reserve. Heat the date sugar. Va tsp salt, 100 ml of water, and vinegar gently in a casserole over medium heat for 3 to 5 minutes until the date sugar is dissolved, then pour over the cucumbers and leave to pickle in the fridge while preparing the tofu.
2. In a large, nonstick frying pan, warm all but 1 tbsp of the oil over medium heat until bubbles start to come to the surface. Add the tofu and fry for 7-10 minutes until the tofu is uniformly golden brown, turning halfway. Remove the tofu

from the pan and place on paper to drain grease.
3. Whisk together the pure maple syrup and miso in a small bowl. Place the sesame seeds on a plate.
4. Brush the tofu with the sticky pure maple syrup sauce and sprinkle with the sesame seeds.
5. Warm the noodles as instructed by the box, then drain and rinse under cold water.
6. Return the frying pan to heat with a little oil, throw in the noodles, and toss.
7. In 4 medium bowls, divide the noodles, tofu, pickled cucumber, spring onion, and some of the miso sauce.
8. Serve immediately.

Nutritional value/servings: Calories: 579; Fat: 20.5g; Saturated fat: 3.5g; Carbohydrate: 77g; Fiber 4g; Sugar 14g; Protein: 21 g; Iron: 4mg; Sodium: 688mg

Southwestern Stuffed Peppers

Prep Time: 30 Minutes ~ Cook Time: 1 Hour 20 Minutes ~ Servings: 4

Ingredients

½ cup low-sodium vegetable broth or 2 teaspoons extra-virgin olive oil for sauteing
1 cup chopped onion
3 garlic cloves, chopped
1 cup uncooked wild rice
1 ½ cups water
4 large red or yellow bell peppers
1 cup frozen com, thawed
1 cup cooked black beans
1/2 teaspoon salt
Freshly ground black pepper
1 (14.5-ounce) can diced tomatoes green chilis, divided

Directions

1. Preheat the oven to 375 °F.
2. In a medium saucepan over medium heat, heat the broth or oil for sauteing. Add the onion and cook until soft and translucent, 4 to 5 minutes. Add the garlic and cook 1 minute more.
3. Add the rice and water. Bring to a boil, then cover and simmer for 30 minutes or until the rice is al dente, adding

more water if needed.
4. Prepare the bell peppers by cutting off the tops and scooping out the seeds and as much of the membranes as you can. Set aside.
5. Put the cooked rice in a large bowl. Add the corn, black beans, salt, pepper, and 1 ½ cups of the diced tomatoes and combine.
6. In the bottom of a medium baking dish, spread the remaining tomatoes. Stand up the peppers in the baking dish and fill them with the rice mixture. Put the tops back on.
7. Cover with foil and bake for 40 minutes. Remove the foil and bake for another 10 minutes.

Nutritional facts: Calories: 308; Fat: 2g; Saturated fat: 0g; Carbohydrate: 65g; Fiber: 11g; Sugar: 13g; Protein: 14g; Iron: 4mg; Sodium: 523mg

Lentil Gumbo

Prep time: 10 minutes ~ Cooking time: 23 minutes ~ Servings: 4

Ingredients

½ tablespoon garlic, diced
½ tablespoon coconut oil
1 bell pepper, chopped
1 celery stalk, chopped
½ teaspoon thyme
teaspoon coriander
1 teaspoon Cajun spices
½ teaspoon white pepper
½ cup lentils
1 ½ cup water

½ cup okra, chopped
1/2 cup tomatoes, diced, canned
1 teaspoon lemon juice
1 oz cauliflower, chopped
1 teaspoon salt

Directions

1. Preheat instant pot on Sauté mode and toss coconut oil inside.
2. Melt it and add bell pepper, garlic, celery stalk, thyme, coriander, and Cajun spices.
3. Mix up the mixture and cook for 10 minutes.
4. Then add all the remaining ingredients except salt.
5. Close and seal the lid.
6. Set Manual mode (high pressure) and cook gumbo for 13 minutes.
7. Then make quick pressure release.
8. Open the lid, add salt, and mix up the meal well.

If you don't have an instant pot, you can cook in your standard pot.

Nutrition value/serving: Calories 129, Fat 2.2, Fiber 9.3, Carbs 20.7, Protein 7.7

Simple Curried Vegetable Rice

Prep Time: 30 Minutes ~ Cooking Time: 10 Minutes ~ Servings: 4

Ingredients

2 cups chopped Carrots
1 cup chopped spinach
2 tsp ginger
1 medium broccoli, chopped
Salt to taste
1 cup cooked Brown Rice
2 cloves garlic, minced
Pepper (to taste)
1 tsp curry Powder

Directions

1. Before you begin cooking, you will want to take some prep time to chop up all of your vegetables beforehand. When they are cut into smaller pieces, this means they will cook faster!
2. Once your ingredients are prepared, take out a pan and begin to heat it over a medium heat. Once warm, add in some olive oil and then sprinkle in the garlic and the gin-
3. Next, you will want to add in the broccoli and carrots. At this point, season with salt and pepper and cook for two minutes.
4. Once the vegetables are cooked to your liking, add in the cooked brown rice along with the curry powder and toss the ingredients until everything is well coated.
5. Finally, add in the spinach and cook for another minute or until it becomes wilted. Season with some more salt and pepper, and then your meal will be ready just like that!

Nutritional facts: Calories: 280 Proteins: 10gCarbs: 50g Fats: 5g

Jen's Cannellini Meatballs with Sun-dried Tomatoes

Prep Time: 20 Minutes ~ Cook Time: 30 Minutes ~ Servings: 4

Ingredients

1/3 cup low-sodium vegetable broth or 2 teaspoons extra-virgin olive oil for sautéing
1/2 cup chopped onion
3 garlic cloves, chopped
1 cup canned cannellini beans, drained and rinsed, aquafaba liquid
1 cup cooked farro
1/4 cup chopped fresh basil, or more
sun-dried tomatoes in oil, drained and coarsely chopped
1/2 teaspoon salt
Freshly ground black pepper
1/2 cup breadcrumbs

Directions

1. Preheat the oven to 375°F. Line a large baking sheet with parchment paper.
2. In a medium sauté pan over medium heat, heat the broth or oil for sauteing. Add the onion and sauté until soft and translucent, 4 to 5 minutes. Add the garlic and cook for another minute.
3. Add the cannellini beans, 2 tablespoons of the aquafaba, farro, basil, onion-garlic mixture, tomatoes, salt, and pepper to a food processor. Pulse a few times until combined. Add

the breadcrumbs and pulse a few more times. (I like it to have a little texture.) Taste and adjust the seasoning if needed. Add another tablespoon aquafaba if you need it to bind more.
4. Scoop out about 2 tablespoons of the mixture and gently form a small ball about 1 1/2 inches in diameter.
5. Place on the baking sheet. Repeat until you have used up the mixture. You will have 10 to 12 meatballs.
6. Bake for 25 minutes, until browned and firm.

Nutritional facts: Calories: 223; Fat: 4g; Saturated fat: 0g; Carbohydrate: 25g; Fiber: 6g; Sugar: 2g; Protein: 9g; Iron: 3mg; Sodium: 387mg

Lentil Steak

Prep time: 10 minutes ~ Cooking time: 8 minutes ~ Servings: 2

Ingredients

1 cup lentils, cooked
1/2 cup bread crumbs
3 tablespoons wheat flour
1 teaspoon salt
1/2 teaspoon chili pepper
1 teaspoon dried oregano
1 tablespoon olive oil

Directions

1. Place lentils into the mixing bowl and mash them with the help of the fork.
2. After this, add wheat flour, salt, chili pepper, and dried oregano.

3. Mix up the mixture until homogenous.
4. With the help of the fingertips, make 2 balls and press them to make steak shape.
5. Preheat instant pot on sauté mode.
6. Then add olive oil.
7. Coat lentil steaks in bread crumbs.
8. Put the steaks in the preheated olive oil.
9. Cook them for 3 minutes from each side or until they are light brown.

Nutrition value/serving: Calories 551, fat 9.7, fiber 31.2, carbs 86.7, protein 29.7

Soups

Spinach and Broccoli Soup

Prep time: 10 minutes ~ Cooking time: 20 minutes ~ Servings: 4

Ingredients

3 shallots, chopped
1 tablespoon olive oil
2 garlic cloves, minced
1/2 pound broccoli florets
1/2 pound baby spinach
salt and black pepper to the taste
3 cups veggie stock
1 teaspoon turmeric powder
1 tablespoon lime juice

Directions

1. Heat up a pot with the oil over medium-high heat, add the shallots and the garlic and sauté for 5 minutes.
2. Add the broccoli, spinach, and the other ingredients, toss, bring to a simmer and cook over medium heat for 15 minutes.
3. Ladle into soup bowls and serve.

Nutritional facts: Calories 150, fat 3, fiber 1, carbs 3, protein 7

Zucchini and Cauliflower Soup

Prep time: 10 minutes ~ Cooking time: 25 minutes ~ Servings: 4

Ingredients

4 scallions, chopped
1 teaspoon ginger, grated
2 tablespoons olive oil
1-pound zucchinis, sliced
2 cups cauliflower florets
salt and black pepper to the taste
2 cups veggie stock
1 garlic clove, minced
1 tablespoon lemon juice
1 cup coconut cream

Directions

1. Heat up a pot with the oil over medium heat, add the scallions, ginger, and the garlic and sauté for 5 minutes.
2. Add the rest of the ingredients, bring to a simmer and cook over medium heat for 20 minutes.
3. Blend everything using an immersion blender, ladle into soup bowls and serve.

Nutritional facts: calories 154, fat 12, fiber 3, carbs 5, protein 4

Double-Garlic Bean and Vegetable Soup

Prep Time: 25 Minutes ~ Cooking time: 10 Minutes ~ Servings: 4

Ingredients

1 tablespoon olive oil
1 teaspoon fine sea salt
1 minced onion
5 cloves garlic, minced
2 cups chopped red potatoes
2/3 cup sliced carrots
1 teaspoon Italian seasoning blend
4 cups water, divided
1 can crushed tomatoes or tomato puree
1 head roasted garlic
2 tablespoons prepared vegan pesto,
plus more for garnish
15 oz. of white beans, drained and rinsed
1-inch (2.5 cm) pieces green beans
salt and pepper

Directions

1. Heat the oil and salt in a large soup pot over medium heat. Add the onion, garlic, potatoes, carrots, and celery. Cook for 4 to 6 minutes, occasionally stirring, until the onions are translucent. Add the seasoning blend, red pepper flakes, and celery seed and stir for 2 minutes. Add 3 cups (705 ml) of the water and the crushed tomatoes.

2. Combine the remaining 1 cup (235 ml) water and the roasted garlic in a blender. Process until smooth. Add to the soup mixture and bring to a boil. Reduce the heat to simmer and cook for 30 minutes.
3. Stir in the pesto, beans, and green beans. Simmer for 15 minutes. Taste and adjust the seasonings.
4. Serve each bowl with a dollop of pesto, if desired.

Nutritional facts: Calories 140, Fat 7, Fiber 14, Carbs 4, Protein 21

Tuscan White Bean Soup

Prep Time: 10 Minutes ~ Cooking tine: 15 Minutes ~ Servings: 4

Ingredients

1 to 2 teaspoons olive oil
1 onion, chopped
4 garlic cloves, minced, or 1 teaspoon garlic powder
2 carrots, peeled and chopped
1 tablespoon dried herbs
Pinch freshly ground black pepper
Pinch red pepper flakes
4 cups vegetable Broth or water
2 (15-ounce) cans white beans, such as cannellini, navy, or great northern, drained and rinsed
2 tablespoons freshly squeezed lemon juice
2 cups chopped greens, such as spinach, kale, arugula, or chard
salt

Directions

1. Heat the olive oil in a large soup pot over medium-high heat. Add the onion, garlic (if using fresh), carrots, and a pinch of salt. Sauté for about 5 minutes, occasionally stirring, until the vegetables are lightly browned. Sprinkle in the dried herbs (plus the garlic powder, if using), black pepper, and red pepper flakes and toss to combine.

2. Add the vegetable broth, beans, and another pinch of salt and bring the soup to a low simmer to heat through. If you like, make the broth a bit creamier by puréeing 1 to 2 cups of soup in a countertop blender and returning it to the pot. Alternatively, use a hand blender to purée about one-fourth of the beans in the pot.
3. Stir in the lemon juice and greens, and let the greens wilt into the soup before

serving. Leftovers will keep in an airtight container for up to 1 week in the refrigerator or up to 1 month in the freezer.

Nutritional facts: Calories: 14 5; Protein: 7g; Total fat: 2g; Saturated fat: 0g; Carbohydrates: 26g; Fiber: 6g

Desserts

Peach Sorbet

Prep Time: 15 Minutes ~ Cooking Time: 0 Minutes ~ Servings: 4

Ingredients

5 peaches, peeled, pitted, and chopped
¾ cup sugar
Juice of 1 lemon or 1 tablespoon prepared lemon juice

Directions

1. In the bowl of a food processor, combine all the ingredients and process until smooth.
2. Pour the mixture into a 9-by-13-inch glass pan. Cover tightly with plastic wrap. Freeze for 3 to 4 hours.
3. Remove from the freezer and scrape the sorbet into a food processor. Process until smooth. Freeze for another

Mixed Berries and Cream

Prep Time: 10 Minutes ~ Cooking Time: 0 Minutes ~ Servings: 4

Ingredients

two 15-ounce cans full-fat coconut milk
3 tablespoons agave
1/2 teaspoon vanilla extract
1 - pint fresh blueberries
2 - pints fresh raspberries
1 - pint fresh strawberries, sliced

Directions

1. Refrigerate the coconut milk overnight. When you open the can, the liquid will have separated from the solids. Spoon out the solids and reserve the liquid for another purpose.
2. In a medium bowl, whisk the agave and vanilla extract into the coconut solids. Divide the berries among four bowls. Top with the coconut cream. Serve immediately.

Lime and Watermelon Granita

Prep Time: 15 Minutes ~ Chilling Time: 6 Minutes ~ Servings: 4

Ingredients

cups seedless watermelon chunks
juice of 2 limes or 2 tablespoons prepared lime juice
1/2 cup sugar
strips of lime zest, for garnish

Directions

1. In a blender or food processor, combine the watermelon, lime juice, and sugar and process until smooth. You may have to do this in two batches. After processing, stir well to combine both batches.
2. Pour the mixture into a 9-by-1 3-inch glass dish. Freeze for 2 to 3 hours.
3. Remove from the freezer and use a fork to scrape the top layer of ice. Leave the shaved ice on top and return to the freezer. In another hour, remove from the freezer and repeat. Do this a few more times until all the ice is scraped up. Serve frozen, garnished with strips of lime zest.

Chocolate Pudding

Prep Time: 5 Minutes ~ Cooking Time: 15 Minutes ~ Servings: 4

Ingredients

1/3 cup sugar
1/3 cup unsweetened cocoa powder
3 cups unsweetened almond milk
1/4 cup cornstarch
pinch of sea salt
1 teaspoon vanilla extract

Directions

1. In a medium bowl, whisk together the sugar and cocoa powder to combine thoroughly. In a large saucepan over medium heat, whisk together the cocoa mixture and 2 1/2 cups of the almond milk. Bring to a boil, stirring constantly. Remove from the heat.
2. In a small bowl, whisk together the remaining 1/2 cup almond milk and cornstarch. Stir into the cocoa mixture and return to medium heat. Add the salt.
3. Stirring constantly, bring the pudding to a boil. It will begin to thicken. Boil for 1 minute. Remove from the heat and stir in the vanilla. Chill before serving.

Coconut and Almond Truffles

Prep Time: 15 Minutes ~ Cooking Time: 0 Minutes ~ Makes 8-10 Truffles

Ingredients

1 cup pitted dates
1 cup almonds
1/2 cup sweetened cocoa powder, plus extra for coating
1/2 cup unsweetened shredded coconut
1/4 cup pure maple syrup
1 teaspoon vanilla extract
1 teaspoon almond extract
1/4 teaspoon sea salt

Directions

1. In the bowl of a food processor, combine all the ingredients and process until smooth. Chill the mixture for about 1 hour.
2. Roll the mixture into balls and then roll the balls in cocoa powder to coat. Serve immediately or keep chilled until ready to serve.

Chocolate Macaroons

Prep Time: 10 Minutes ~ Cooking Time: 15 Minutes ~ Makes 8 To 10 Macaroons

Ingredients

1 cup unsweetened shredded coconut
2 tablespoons cocoa powder
2/3 cup coconut milk
1/4 cup agave
pinch of sea salt

Directions

1. Preheat the oven to 350°F. Line a baking sheet with parchment paper. In a medium saucepan, cook all the ingredients over medium-high heat until a firm dough is formed.
2. Scoop the dough into balls and place them on the baking sheet. Bake for 15 minutes, remove from the oven and let cool on the baking sheet.
3. Serve cooled macaroons or store in a tightly sealed container for up to 1 week.

Conclusion

"One to change a few. A few to change many. Many to change the world. Starts with one." – Anonymous

Indeed, a plant-based diet is only plant-based products.

There are no meats, dairy, fish, or eggs included.

While a plant-based diet is relatively rare, the truth is that they are quickly becoming more common. Numerous people choose it for health or philosophical reasons - such as not wanting to harm animals or for sustainability.

Before you can really transition into a plant-based diet with confidence and increase your chances of success, you must learn to educate yourself on why you are considering it in the first place.

Whatever your reason for choosing a plant-based diet, the most important thing is for you to educate yourself before you get started. That is why this book is tailored just for you - to give you all the information you need about a plant-based diet, including all the do's and don'ts and the tips and tricks to help you make the most of this diet.

When you learn the benefits of a plant-based diet, how to make it a lifestyle, and how other people out there have done it, you will be focused on making it work for you too. When you know why you are going plant-based, it will open your eyes, motivate you, and get you excited about it - all of which are key to achieving success.

The trick is to focus on crowding out rather than cutting out. When you approach a plant-based diet from an angle of crowding out animal products with tons of delicious, filling plant-based food options, everything becomes seamless and fun. Go for nondairy milk, whole grains, veggies, fruits, seeds, nuts, and legumes to get started on a plant-based diet. Try as much as you can to stay away from vegan replacement meats.

Look out for simple recipe inspirations and try them out. You will likely have all the required ingredients in your pantry. Most of your favorite recipes that you are already cooking and love can be turned into vegan/plant-based versions. Put it simply - you just have to remove the meat, cheese, milk, etc. These days you will find a lot of alternatives in your supermarket, from tofu to fake meat.

Now that you have recipes for your plant-based diet, the next thing is for you to go out shopping for the right vegan foods. The best thing is for you to buy all the vegan food you can get your hands on. Ensure that you stock up your pantry with as much produce as you possibly can - including healthy grains like wild rice, quinoa, and oats.

When you are learning to transition into a plant-based diet, you must learn not to overwhelm yourself. You don't have to make your meals complicated or cook them in a gourmet style. The trick is to take everything easy and count each day as it comes.

Finally, find a plant-based or vegan community that can support you on this journey. When you surround yourself with like-minded people, you will not only feel protected but also motivated to be yourself and have some fun while at it.

www.ingramcontent.com/pod-product-compliance
Lightning Source LLC
Chambersburg PA
CBHW071440070526
44578CB00001B/172